REFLECTIVE THINKING IN SOCIAL WORK

It is vital that social work students learn to integrate their personal and professional selves if they are to meet the challenges of social work in complex changing environments. This accessible text is designed to enable readers to explore and build on their existing skills and abilities, supporting them to become competent and self-aware reflective practitioners.

Reflective Thinking in Social Work uses stories told by a range of social work students to model reflective practice learning. Discussing issues such as identity, motivation to enter the social work profession and lived experiences in the journey into social work, the book brings together stories of hardship, privilege, families, hopes, interests and community activism from many diverse ethnic backgrounds. Each narrative is introduced by the author and ends with a commentary drawing out the key themes and exploring how the reader can use the narrative to enhance their own understanding and critical thinking, and to engage in transformative practice.

Framed by an in-depth discussion of available frameworks for reflective practice in different contexts and the importance of narratives in constructing identities, this is an invaluable text for social work students at both bachelor's and master's degree levels.

Mekada Julia Graham is Professor and Chair in Social Work at California State University, Dominguez Hills, USA.

REFLECTIVE THINKING IN SOCIAL WORK

Learning from student narratives

Mekada Julia Graham

Routledge
Taylor & Francis Group

LONDON AND NEW YORK

First published 2017
by Routledge
2 Park Square, Milton Park, Abingdon, Oxon OX14 4RN

and by Routledge
711 Third Avenue, New York, NY 10017

Routledge is an imprint of the Taylor & Francis Group, an informa business

British Library Cataloguing in Publication Data
A catalogue record for this book is available from the British Library

Library of Congress Cataloging in Publication Data
A catalog record for this title has been requested

ISBN: 978-1-138-77901-3 (hbk)
ISBN: 978-1-138-77902-0 (pbk)
ISBN: 978-1-315-77157-1 (ebk)

Typeset in Bembo
by Taylor & Francis Books

Dedicated to Mum and Dad, Kira Mary, Louis and Kayden

CONTENTS

Foreword   *ix*
Acknowledgements   *xi*

PART I
Narrative, reflection, personal stories and research   **1**

1 Introduction   3

2 Reflective learning to critical reflection: models and background
   stories   30

3 Research, narrative, reflection and self-inquiry   55

PART II
Student narratives   **75**

Introducing student narratives   77

4 The voice of my journey (Vanessa Correa)   81

5 Reflecting critically on my journey through social work
   education in an Australian university (Tejaswini Patil and
   Michelle Moss)   88

6 Narrative about my journey through social work education
   (Frida Svensson)   98

7 Unending expedition: a reflective account of my journey to the
   social work profession (Yogita Naruka)   105

8 Reflective narrative (Layla Sewell)   112

9 My journey through social work education (Nicole Jones)   118

10 My narrative (Anthony Constantino)   125

11 A gift to a student social worker (Anna Marie Monck)   130

12 Final comments   137

Index   139

FOREWORD

It is often said that use of self is the single most important characteristic of any professional practice. The craft, artistry and style of social work practice engagements rely on our ability to mobilize, review and consider aspects of self in the context of the helping relationship and deploy strong critical reflection. The notion of reflective thinking is deeply embedded in social work practice. Reflection is regarded as core to the development of the professional self inasmuch as it is acknowledged that we are implicated in what we do and how we do it. None of this is new. The centrality of self in social work is as old as the hills. However, understandings of self and how it is articulated and the theorizing of reflectiveness have developed apace and in many directions, and these extensions of the literature are worthy of critical interrogation. *Reflective Thinking in Social Work: Learning from student narratives* is grounded in such a review, guiding us through models of reflection and associated concepts as the gateway into a consideration of the personal reflections and narratives that make up this body of work. The book unravels a series of complex and intertwined concepts arising from various theoretical positions including subjectivity, reflexivity, agency and identity, and, interestingly, the emotional work of reflective practice. These in turn contribute to our understanding of the relationship between reflection in action, between theory and practice.

The book's orchestrating assertion is that narratives of self and our related critical reflections are located in the context of historical, social, cultural and political considerations; forces that influence and structure not only our articulations of self – the personal story – but shape how these are or can be performed. It is this insistence on the validity of ways of being in the world that distinguishes this text and renders it so refreshing to the social work reader. These are not simply personal stories but personal stories that have political import, collective import and which grapple with the connections to be made between the personal and the professional. Mekada steers the book with her own narrative, demonstrating an authoring of the text that is based on an honest, open and trustful exchange with the contributors. This underpinning methodology for the text shines throughout and enables a rich exploration of personal journeys towards the development of professional identities.

Everyone loves a story. The deployment of narratives in social science research and practice has risen in popularity in recognition both of the authenticity that lived experience brings to the development of knowledge(s) and in terms of the therapeutic value of storytelling both to the teller and to the audience. Usefully the book explores the use of narratives in research before turning to the educational import. The application of auto-ethnography to stories of student transitions in education is novel, fascinating and instructive. Rarely do we hear the voice of students and rarely is their voice as well-articulated as in this rich collection which gives insights into their motivations, fears, aspirations and observations on their professional transitions. The range and diversity of the stories fascinates and gives the book international appeal. Mekada has gathered accounts from across the world that speak to the diversity of social work practice but also to the coherence of the professional enterprise and value base. Their use in learning and teaching is guaranteed as is their relevance to all practice-based disciplines.

We know from practice accounts that such reflective space has been severely curtailed in the hustle and bustle of day-to-day practice and in no small measure undermined by the exigencies of neoliberal methodologies. We have lost those moments of contemplative consideration and consequently there has been an impoverishment of practice both for the worker and for the service user. This text revitalizes and relocates this endeavor as central to good practice, as part of student training and as critical to continuous professional development. As such, it makes a very valuable contribution to the field.

Charlotte Williams, Professor of Social Work and Deputy Dean, RMIT University, Melbourne, Australia, and author of *Sugar and Slate* (2002)

ACKNOWLEDGEMENTS

A special thank you to Dr. Maria Avila for being my discussion partner on many issues surrounding reflective practice, personal stories and narrative approaches. Dr. Avila supported my book project throughout its development.

I am grateful to the College of Health, Human Services and Nursing here at Dominguez Hills for their encouragement and assistance in completing the manuscript during the busy Fall semester of 2015. The book includes some of my research about teaching, critical theory and student journeys through social work education and I obtained Institutional Review Board research protocols in this regard. I appreciate the support and encouragement of Grace McInnes, commissioning editor, Louise Vahtrick and Shannon Kneis as this project progressed allowing for an extension to complete the book.

Some of the thoughts included in my story in Chapter 1 appeared in an earlier version. I am grateful to the publishers for permission to extract and use in this book parts from 'From London to California: A journey in social work education,' in V. Cree (ed.), *Becoming a Social Worker: Narratives from Around the World*, London, Routledge, 2013.

I would like to thank my best friend and life partner, Julian, for his ongoing support, encouragement and humor through the writing process.

Finally, I would like to thank my many students over the years and the narrative contributions from students at California State University Dominguez Hill here in Los Angeles as well as students in England, Australia, India and Sweden.

PART I

Narrative, reflection, personal stories and research

1

INTRODUCTION

Reflective practice learning in social work has taken center stage in recent years, applying various models for students to engage in reflections on and in practice across different contexts and situations. This interest in reflection is not only confined to the world of social work but rather is a key teaching and learning strategy in other practice disciplines including teaching, medicine, occupational therapy, nursing and adult education. Even though there is a lack of agreed upon definitions of reflective practice and how these activities might be researched, these strategies are deemed essential in developing knowledge for practice and professional life. Whereas much attention has been paid to these core practice developments, others have promoted the transformative qualities of reflective practice to craft a kind of knowing in action which examines the social, cultural and political contexts of learning and practice (Lyons, 2010).

The 'reflective turn' coined by Schön (1991) is not only driven by the importance of reflection in social work practice but also its intrinsic capacity for self-awareness and a sense of self in helping relationships. These threads of self-awareness weave an intersecting web of professional life-long learning often through writing ourselves into practice. Reflection has become an important part of learning to become a social worker, through various processes, which invite students and professionals to question their understandings and beliefs about how the world works, locating ourselves in context. This learning model is based upon our active involvement through a journey of discovery, problem solving and linking the realities of practice experience with creative action strategies (Cooper, 2006).

Developing skills and abilities through this reflective process is the first step to becoming a competent reflective practitioner. This is not an easy task in a demanding and busy world of social work practice, yet this is when we need to make increasing effort to be reflective using a 'reflective space' to think about expectations, priorities and managing pressures of work, education and best use of time (Clutterbuck, 2001). It is all very well to talk about reflection even in our professional lives when the hectic pace of day-to-day work leaves little opportunity to notice or find these spaces and we often stick to routines as a way of coping with heavy workloads. The journey towards being and doing reflective practice are often beset with bumps and setbacks along the way through social work education and beyond. The process involves personal growth through the development of emotional capacities, focus on self and lived experiences, openness to life's possibilities and to be aware of our own biases and preferences.

Our personal histories and experience shape our thinking and assumptions that underlie our thoughts and actions. Questions come up about how our personal history and culture have impacted the way we interact with others; thinking about the ways in which all aspects of the human self and everyday environments affect our choices of modality in practice. Reflective practice prompts questions about what we know and why – in other words, how we come to know it. Being reflective requires us to examine our own meaning-making processes. What we see and understand in a situation is influenced by our 'subjectivity' including our embodiment – for example, gender, ethnicity, social location, age, sexual orientation and ability. As practitioners, we do not simply collect 'facts' in a neutral fashion about people and their 'problems'; we are implicated in the work we are engaged in, constructing versions of cases and in this sense making knowledge about clients (Fook, 2012).

In writing the preface to *Guided Reflection*, Johns (2010: vii–viii), comments on the reflective turn and its movement into a narrative turn, 'marking a distinction between representing lived experience as narrative to presenting it as performance … narrative is not primarily an intellectual inquiry pursuit. Rather, it is a genuine endeavour to become better at what we seek to do.' These comments bring together reflection and narrative, weaving a pattern of knowing and self-inquiry. The concept of narrative is often equated interchangeably with stories and their structures as a way of transforming lived experiences into meaning. Polkinghorne (1988: 18) considers narrative as 'a meaning structure that organizes events and human actions into a whole, thereby attributing significance to individual actions and events according to their effect on the whole.' The stories we tell about our lives knit together with our evolving identities, embracing our lives in various ways. The past decades have witnessed a growing interest in all aspects of narrative with an increase in the number of conferences and seminars bringing together researchers from a range of disciplines in the humanities and social sciences. Despite this interest, there is no consensus on a definition of narrative and in any case it seems no definition will fit all approaches to narrative existing in various places. Perhaps it is safe to say that there are many meanings attached to narrative depending upon its use in different disciplines and contexts.

The way this book is organized

There is no shortage of literature on reflection as a framework for students to engage in reflective learning covered in this book. However, what this book does offer is a range of perspectives and connections across social work, reflection, critical practice, narrative and personal story. Taking these themes on board, the book is organized into two distinct parts, with the first three chapters exploring reflective practice, social work, research and self-inquiry within the context of narrative. In Part II, Chapters 4 to 11 focus on student narratives which include personalized and detailed passages about identities, lived experiences often within the context of social justice, empowerment, journeys through and within social work education and child welfare.

In this Chapter I introduce my own story and insights from life experiences as a contribution to my pathway of reflection and self-inquiry. I also believe a story can be judged as valuable in its own right as a learning construct bringing academic ideas and narrative approaches to the world of social work practice. Many have advocated that our personal stories and lived experiences include elements of cultural and social narratives linking reflection with a deeper sense of self. Later in this chapter I describe a student exchange Skype project in which students in social work programs in London and Los Angeles shared different ideas and points of view about the nuts and bolts of social work practice in both localities. In addition, I have included excerpts from podcasts shared among students[1] about their backgrounds, identities and motivations to pursue a career in social work as resources for reflection and practice work. This outline gives a valuable context to the rest of the book.

In Chapter 2, I explore the nature of reflection, reflective practice and links with critical theory and practice. Just as there are many definitions surrounding notions of professionalism, this is the case for reflection and reflective practice. I draw on the work of a range of authors, including Fook and Schön, amongst others, to open up evolving debates about critical reflection and professional practice. This section continues with the interplay of reflection, critical theory and postmodern approaches and their influence on forms of social work practice. The final sections of the chapter include the changing dynamics of anti-discriminatory/oppressive models and their applications in a postmodern framework, as well as emotional aspects of reflection.

In Chapter 3, my interest moves to qualitative research where emerging developments have constructed approaches that embrace different media, many derived from the humanities. Narrative research has been referred to as a 'field in the making' since it invites attention to experiences that other research approaches are unable to reveal (Clough, 2002). With reference to authors in the field, this chapter presents a brief overview of qualitative research and social work, tracing emerging forms of narrative research. In many ways, narrative research has resonance with social work's social justice ambitions because it involves stories from the ground up in collaboration with the researcher often working in tandem to ensure marginalized voices are heard. This research practice highlights lived experience in context, thereby opening up new lines of inquiry and possibilities. Forms of narrative inquiry pay attention to how we make sense of human experiences and learning that emerge from these experiences. I also look at auto-ethnography which allows researchers to write themselves into research using a participatory frame of reference. Through this experience, researchers find themselves in the middle of evolving stories together with becoming aware of their own learning about narrative. These self-reflection activities provide important forms of narrative offering a platform for developing skills of critique about one's professional practice. With attention to everyday life, interactions can signify sites for the exercise of and indeed resistance to the power of dominant discourses. In all, this chapter briefly touches on the wide-range set of activities in narrative research and links with reflective practice and critical social work.

In Part II of the book, I introduce a collection of student narratives from around the world, including India, Sweden, England, Australia and here at California State University Dominguez Hills (CSUDH). Throughout Part I, I make reference to these narratives to encourage readers to delve into this part of the book, taking the first three chapters as the landscape and vista into the ways in which we experience the world as storytellers.

In Chapters 4–11, the narratives are loosely linked separately through the themes of identities, social justice, empowerment, child welfare and journeys through social work education. The narratives are not prescribed, they follow a tentative path, organized around this set of themes, some of which were outlined in my call for narratives and some influenced by their work in critical race studies, an anti-racist framework incorporated into a critical social work course. Each narrative is presented separately and represents a journey and reflective space where students consider their experiences. I encouraged students 'to talk about how I felt' and in this way bring to life the personal and social past in the present (Ellis, 1993: 720). The narratives open up a reflective space for readers to think about their own experiences in the field or through education to encourage dialogue and learning. Rather than taking the narratives apart, the purpose here is to think with and through stories as a unified whole (Herrmann and DiFate, 2014). Simply put, there are commonalities between experiences as well as layers of complexity located in various contexts. This process involved students being able to acknowledge the way their own values, assumptions and interpretations have influenced their construction of stories. One of the contributions of postmodern approaches is the encouragement of representations of 'realities' and the role of personal voice in writing about lived experiences. These narrative sources carve out forms of communication to create meaningful dialogue with readers. I do hope that these narratives are not only read by individuals but also are used to provoke useful discussions about motivations, values, purpose and commitments in classrooms and other settings. These stories can be particularly valuable in field and research seminars in initiating reflection, perhaps illuminating hidden avenues of thought and action. In thinking about these learning stories, we catch a glimpse of lived experiences in a particular time and context to mull over conversations about the meaning and significance of reflection connecting personal stories of self in places where developing reflective practice and self-study hold a central place. The final comments pick up themes of the book and return to questions about narrative, personal story, reflection and critical practice.

Writing this book

My motivation in writing this book emerged through my teaching and academic research as a faculty member in the Department of Social Work at CSUDH in Los Angeles. My experiences of teaching students over many years have brought me to this point with the intention of exploring the possibilities of critical social work and reflection, and perhaps more importantly through learning stories from student narratives. Most of my academic research has centered upon what can be loosely described as oppression studies through the frame of critical theory.

As I write this introduction, I have considered why a book about narratives? What is it about narratives that I am drawn to in this moment? I can think of two reasons that come to mind. First, histories of narrative as voice in telling of lived experiences continue to be pivotal in galvanizing social and political movements for civil and human rights. In many other ways I have always enjoyed reading about people's lived experiences in both historical and contemporary fiction and non-fiction. I am attracted to these intellectual and fiction works and spend time reading about life as it is lived in different locations and social environments. Second, although social work and social welfare have been my main fields of inquiry, narrative is broad enough to engage across my interests in other disciplines. I want to extend my knowledge of narrative inquiry to unravel puzzles, unknowns and questions in this evolving field. What better way to start than write a book? In all this, I am, as are many others, interested in how people make sense of the world around them and connect meaning to their lives. As Bold (2012: 13) explains, 'I believe that narratives of various kinds help people to construct and understand their social world.' It is through narratives that social and cultural constructs are communicated as a means of reality giving importance to subjective meaning and emotion. I have a sense of wanting to know more about how things work in the social world and particularly entrenched social divisions impacting individuals and families, their life chances and daily lives.

In this opening chapter I want to set the scene and context, so to speak, for this project on reflective thinking and student narratives. Initially, as I was sketching out the chapters of this book, I noticed that in this writing, the book moved along in different directions than I envisaged. Some of the shifts in direction came about in wanting to write myself into the text, and steering it along with this in mind I found to be challenging because in many ways this work is also about my own life story and journey of self-inquiry. In writing and reflecting about my own story I was struck by its links with prior experiences and emotions, some of which steered reflections about what I should leave out and what would be 'okay' in the book for everyone to see. My first step into the 'personal' in public writing pushed me to reflect upon my story as a speaking of experience and telling of a story; a narrative of oneself that could be placed alongside other narratives (Healy and Leonard, 2000). Of course, experiences are not lived or necessarily reflected upon in an orderly fashion with neat beginnings and endings; they are a series of evolving, complex, contradictory narratives. The story is simply a glimpse into a series of unfolding experiences (Johns, 2010).

The process of accessing experiences can be a daunting task sitting at a computer waiting for experiences to appear to tell a story, recapturing an event in the moment, bringing all the senses to bear through the writing. It was almost as if I needed the security of a template to guide me and offer some kind of structure – a safer way, a more familiar way I am used to in my academic writing. In any case, while an academic format is not entirely discounted, I wanted to allow for a personal style, one which is more in tune with narrative. The experience of letting the words flow into their own creation was shrouded in contradictory feelings like dipping your toe into uncharted waters as the personal is written into the text. Although I wanted to be present in this project, I had to reassure myself that people tell their stories as best they can and in this postmodern era knowledge is diverse with new forms of research and understanding of the social world. In writing about my own experiences and placing them into stories, this telling is part of a process of revealing myself to myself as I continue to dialogue with self-inquiry in tentative ways. There were many stops and starts along the way as well as pauses before moving back on track.

Although I have not been able to develop all the areas as I would have liked, it is apparent to me through the process of writing this book that I have a clearer understanding of my own personal story through connections with education as a transformative experience; structural forces and relations of power; critical reflection, narrative in a wider cultural sense and student narratives. In writing this book, I hope to have achieved a style that the readers, albeit students in social work, human services, practitioners or social work educators, will find useful and accessible. This book includes references to work in other fields besides social work. I wanted to show wider connections with studies of changing experiences and different outlooks of individuals in their daily lives as well as glean insights from a range of sources. As I moved along, writing the chapters, I became more aware of developments in other disciplines and their relevance to this book project.

During my years of working with students, I have found that students often choose to study social work coupled with notions about wanting to help others. This desire to help others is sometimes framed by simplistic ideas about social justice and how the world can be changed for the better. On the surface, understanding students' motivations seems a reasonable way to indicate how they will approach this work. Yet it is a more complicated story involving not only this choice of career but also steeped in personal and social contexts as well as time and place. It is clear that when students engage the realities of social work practice, their experiences often run counter to their expectations and daily experiences of practitioners in the field. Not surprisingly, social work educators currently place even more emphasis on preparation for practice and guidance as students grapple with integrating personal and professional aspects of self in becoming a practitioner.

Through writing this book, I want to bring student voices through narratives into the ever-growing literature and interest in reflective thinking and practice. Rather than writing about the whys and wherefores of reflective practice and how to engage in this process, I wanted to illuminate a narrative approach through my own story together with student stories as experiential, holding a vision of self and practice (Johns, 2010). My interests are to explore three connecting themes – critical reflection, narrative and life stories – to better understand their relationship in social work theory, practice and research. This approach appeals to me because it offers readers the opportunity to learn directly from stories and views from students themselves. In the call for student narratives, I asked questions about what students have to say about their journeys in and through social work education, their identities and motivation to enter the profession of social work. I also requested that students connect these themes with their personal stories.

Of course, this book is also closely connected with my experiences as a social work educator, teaching students in the Department of Social Work in CSUDH. Conversely, the university has its own story located in its beginnings connected with civil rights movements in the heady days of the 1960s. In the aftermath of the 1965 Watts riots in Los Angeles, surrounding communities advocated for a public university for their young people and so this is how Dominguez Hills was created. This rich history is testament to the vision of surrounding communities to bring about social change through higher education and beyond. The university is surrounded by both low-income communities (including Compton) as well as better-resourced areas, and is perceived as offering much needed opportunities for people to gain undergraduate and graduate degrees in pursuing professional careers.

During my first year as a faculty member at the university, I visited several museums and attended other activities located in surrounding communities. Conversations along the way, helped by interest in my English accent, often shifted to education and the importance of Dominguez Hills as not only the hub for many community, educational and other activities, but also a place that offered hope and possibilities in higher education for mainly low-income working-class communities. The campus educates the most ethnically and racially diverse student body (Latino, African American, European American, Asian or Pacific Islander, Native American and multiple ethnicities) in the USA. Social class is one area these social groups have in common and they are often confronted by historical prejudices, whilst others experience discrimination because of language barriers and immigration status. Many students entering the graduate social work program here are first-generation college graduates and come from the surrounding communities and beyond.

I have had a longstanding interest in critical social work practice, incorporating anti-racist and feminist perspectives as well as indigenous ways of knowing and understanding the social world. Initially, my interest in this project began at the University of Salford, near Manchester, UK, in 2012, where I attended a seminar joined by social work educators from around the UK to discuss the changing landscape of anti-racist social work practice and its demise in national contexts as well as gaps between anti-racist theory/perspectives and what was happening on the practice floor. There were lively discussions about the current state of play, particularly in welfare arrangements linked to policies embracing an individualized and free-market approach as the best way to achieve human well-being. Against this background, managerial approaches have dominated day-to-day social work practice requiring more attention to targets, driving increased paperwork, procedures and budgets.

Another conversation took place about changing demographics and the nature of ethnic diversity, particularly in cities around the UK. Migrants from within the European Union as well as other parts of the world have joined long-settled minority communities. Vertovec's (2008) phrase 'superdiversity' comes to mind, where diversity within diversity highlights the sheer complexity of the contemporary scene. Sitting beside these developments are new and emerging ethnicities including a growing dual heritage and multi-ethnic populations and intersections of culture across transnational boundaries. Certainly, the changing demographics surrounding superdiversity have opened up a more nuanced understanding of the complexities surrounding race and ethnicity resulting in questions about anti-racist and anti-discriminatory practice and the current state of play. It was clear that the gap between theory and the realities of practice continued to raise concerns. It seems as if there is nothing more to say about anti-racist practice in Britain or race equality in the USA since these issues have been subsumed into models of equality of oppressions or mainstreamed in legislation and policy developments (Graham and Schiele, 2010). There are some similarities in the demographics of Los Angeles and certainly superdiversity characterizes the contemporary scene here. Our discussions turned to social work students and our role as social work educators in identifying some of the barriers to effective anti-racist and confident race equality practice. In what ways can practice be improved through infusing critical theory and reflection from the ground up in the daily experience of clients and practitioners as listeners and learners?

In offering my experience in teaching and interacting with students, I shared my interest in understanding more about how students viewed their journey through social work education, and constructed connections between personal troubles and broader social issues in practice. More specifically, how structural limitations, social contexts and challenges contributed to difficulties experienced by individuals, families and communities, and how students linked these issues with their own lives, social conditions and communities. In turn, these accounts facilitated conversations about how histories and dominant narratives might shape thinking, feeling and talk about themselves in given ways. Of course, unearthing individual stories often reveals connections with dominant cultural narratives or stories students are familiar with in cultural and social contexts. These familiar narratives can be both positive and negative, even at the same time depending upon multiple perspectives, yet they are socially constructed, often categorizing groups in particular ways. Questions arise about how students find means and strengths to challenge these scripts to write new stories embedded in experiential ways. These evolving narratives of self mesh the personal and public worlds, intimate and wider social experiences, past, present and future (West, 1996).

As I learned more about students' backgrounds and their communities, I began to reflect upon their efforts to enter higher education and a graduate program; their lived experiences; their stories as they embarked on their journey through social work. I have been often inspired by the stories students write and tell about their lived experiences and through their stories I have learned more about the world. Looking back, I realize that these stories have influenced my teaching and academic work as the retelling of these experiences provides a way of understanding life as it is lived. These experiences and events informed my interest in narrative inquiry to learn about the best way to develop critical social work and skills for reflective thinking and practice.

The almost dogged professional steer towards reflective practice as the vehicle for learning about practice has prompted greater understanding of the challenges in teaching critical reflection, theory and practice. I have grappled with these challenges identified by many others, of how to address the '-isms' located in structural social, political and economic contexts into the daily messy world of practice that engage students in a meaningful way (Fook, 2012; Morley, 2008). My specific challenges include unfamiliar divisions between macro and micro practice (a common separation of practice in social work literature), which has felt more rigid and in some ways more divisive in US 'social work cultures' than I am used to. Some of these divisions, I am sure, are explained through the much broader array of agencies and institutions offering career opportunities in social work, including leadership and administration roles as CEOs of large non-profit organizations, in employee assistance programs (providing counseling and mediation services), community organizing and capacity building, policy areas in state and federal government, working in local jails, therapeutic services in various agencies, in universities counseling students and employees. I have experienced different 'cultures' of social work in Europe and the USA shaped by local and national contexts inextricably linked to broader socio-politics and economics of social welfare as well as the status and positioning of the social work profession itself.

In thinking about teaching critical practice, Morley (2008) points out the traditional banking of knowledge approach is replaced by a more reflective stance, one in which student learning engages in dialogue and interaction framed by postmodern approaches in understanding the social world. In reflecting upon these challenges, I found Morley's (2008: 409) reflective account of experiences in teaching critical and reflective practice as a form of resistance supportive in opening up these possibilities of dialogue and interaction. She writes:

> I don't want to see that students can display empathy because they have learnt how to model an empathic response. I need to see the students develop a genuine empathic response through their critical analysis and appreciation of the social and political context of clients' experiences. Such an analysis has clear implications for orientating social work practice towards progressive social change ideals.

Moving to my personal story

During this writing process I felt it was important to provide some background to readers to help them understand personal experiences by introducing myself through this encounter in context as a way of finding my own voice. This was not an easy process. Yet, in the process of looking back over life experiences and events, connections were often made between them, bringing more thoughts and arousing further questions along the way. Through my reading of literature about narrative and making connections with my own life, I have become deeply attached to the notion that the stories we tell are situated in particular contexts and our stories are about our many selves (Hyvarinen, 2008). This reflective space held layers of possibilities to consider my own experiences and dwell on the complexities and contradictions as I followed this path. In writing personal stories, Ellis (1993) explains that telling, writing and reflecting on your own story helps in understanding better the position from which you speak now in this and all academic work. Writing can be a way of knowing as a method of discovery – not as a manufactured process but rather as a journey through which learning can take place. I struggled with the idea of looking at self as a study in and of itself, self-inquiry coming to know that I am because of my story.

I wanted to introduce myself at an early stage, as this project is a personal journey as well as an academic project. I grappled with narrative and story, its purpose and standing in academic circles, even though postmodern approaches have given prominence to experiential knowledge and the power of 'voice' immersed in the world of others. Danto (2008: 719) places voice as a reflection of identity 'constructed by layers of gender, race, class, age and historical context,' and in this way our stories are shaped by these social characteristics subject to historical times, social and political contexts. It is all about the 'personal' involving writing in the first person, often discouraged in traditional inquiry; moreover, its value is often subject to greater scrutiny in academic work. More recently there has been a gradual opening up to a personal style in academic circles; still, an author who is 'too present' in text is often frowned upon (Cihodariu, 2012). There are other struggles – not just about the place of narrative and stories in academic work but also doubts about naming your own discomforts and laying bare your own story in public writing. It is all very well, writing your own story with purpose of insight and growth; nonetheless, thoughts, strong emotions and feelings come together sometimes in unexpected ways. As I have thought more about this practice, I have come to appreciate that life stories involve others, and in this way our stories are also other people's stories. These stories become a framework for examining and interpreting our own personal and cultural experiences (Johns, 2010).

Interestingly my first encounter with a personalized style of writing came about on one of my trips back to England. I met with my colleague and friend, Vivienne Cree, and she asked me to write a chapter in her edited book entitled *Becoming a Social Worker: Global Narratives* (2013). I experienced this process as I thought carefully about writing this chapter, and at some points I hesitated at the thought of writing about incidents that were difficult or uncomfortable as part of my story. I am not alone in this zone of discomfort, as Ellis (2004) recounts this experience as well. She narrates her own struggles with issues of writing particularly in relation to family members, and asks questions about whether and how to examine her own personal stories. In a similar way, she comments that this kind of writing usually involves some kind of emotional turmoil and vulnerability through the interrogation of self and telling what you find. As we can see, this is part and parcel of bringing the 'I' into research and writing. Narrative writing sometimes 'requires our willingness to be uncomfortable … along the way,' bringing the personal and emotional aspects of narrative writing together, which means 'giving up the notion that our work should protect us from the pain and difficulty of living' (Ellis, 1993: 727).

Even though this project involves open and frank discussions with the self, I began writing with a sense of joy and optimism in recounting my motivations and journey into social work, which was probably, as for many others, a roundabout way of landing a university place, taking a four-year degree course together with a qualification in social work. Of course, motivations and why we entered the profession are subject to change at different times as we move along career paths. I know for me, social work was not my first choice and I wanted to become a teacher partly because I was unsure about the kinds of work social workers carried out, apart from 'looked after' children taken into the care system. Looking back, a career in social work can be seen through the lens of our experiences coupled with other things happening in our lives at particular times. Healy and Leonard (2000: 26) reiterate this statement, which is mentioned earlier in this section, saying 'our interpretations are profoundly shaped by different contexts of time, space and experiences.'

Here are parts of my story, some of which are derived from the chapter mentioned earlier. In many ways, looking back, my journey into higher education seems improbable given my background. As I engage in this writing I see that I have been able to step away from places I was expected to inhabit through circumstance to places no one expected me to be, most of all myself, in life's twists and turns. I was born in east London and spent my early years living with my young parents in Cable Street in Whitechapel. I decided to take a look at the history of Cable Street on the internet to see what it was like many years ago. What I found is that in the past this area was referred to as a moral blot on the landscape of London, known for its brothels, cheap lodgings, pubs and drugs through Victorian times to the 1950s. It was also well known for the 'battle of Cable Street,' when people fought to prevent a march by the Blackshirts, Nazi sympathizers, in a mainly Jewish area in the 1930s. It was still a difficult area of London to live in during the 1950s, when poverty and substandard housing were the norm. My parents moved to north London to live first with my grandfather, aunt and her family for several years, and then with my siblings in a prefabricated council house[2] (social housing of the time).

The primary school I attended introduced me to the local library, which became an important place to me. This is where I discovered my love of books; the joy of reading and wonderful stories often about children living in boarding schools and having exciting and comfortable lives. It was also an escape to dream about life's possibilities particularly on a rainy Saturday afternoon! This was my entry to the world of reading and in many ways these early experiences have stayed with me throughout my life. I made weekly visits on my own or with my siblings, reading mostly fiction, and then on Saturday mornings to watch films and cartoons at the Gaumont cinema, which was almost next door.

I grew up in a working-class area, where a lack of finances was a fact of life, although this is something I became aware of as I grew older. My grandfather supported our family in so many different ways. He managed to secure a permanent job as a chauffeur in a government department in postwar Britain and although he left school at the age of 14, he had a love of reading, education and politics (the Labour Party) generally, which I think fueled his ongoing upbeat optimism and the future lives we would inherit. He had sets of encyclopedias and subscribed to Reader's Digest. He held great store in the future of nuclear energy and technological advances which he attributed to the USA that would generate free electricity and somehow create a better world for everyone.

As a child of mixed heritage[3] I experienced racism in my school years. My mother was white English and my father was Cuban, who came to London during the late 1940s. I have strong memories of growing up and like many others with very mixed experiences in my school life. I made some great friends but, on the other hand, in the rough and tumble of the school playground I was frequently the butt of hurtful and bullying behavior by my classmates. I sometimes found these experiences very distressing and remember running home on one occasion during the school day and my mother accompanying me back to school the following day. As a child, people would often ask me which country I was from, followed by assumptions about my 'enjoyment' of warm weather in summer. They seemed perplexed when I replied I was born in London and lived down the road. Reflecting on this experience, at the time, I felt uncomfortable and confused about the questions asked about where I was from. This was perhaps my first introduction to social constructionism and later left me wondering about my status as 'other.' Later, as I grew up I defined myself as British, although I was born in England. Over time 'Englishness' has often been associated with 'whiteness' linked to a generational past, and everyone else born in the UK can take British status because it is related to the British Empire, its colonial past and people of color. Social constructivism has given me the language for this experience and I am able to see the way in which my identity is deeply influenced by my social location. Living as I do at this time, in another country, it has been somewhat easier to shape my own identity about who I am and social location, with a sense of interpreting this earlier experience in another way helped by a different social, political and geographical location.

In this space of thinking and reflecting on my own efforts to obtain a university education brought memories of my first job at 16 years old as a junior assistant (a great title for a 'go for' – i.e. go and get my lunch, cigarettes and make the tea), and the assistance of my boss, a young, well-educated (University of Cambridge) woman in her twenties, in helping me to recognize my potential. My job was in a publishing house on a magazine about parenting and young children. Acquiring this job was beset with experiences of discrimination. After my interview, the editor said she wanted me to start the following week. She told me to go to the Personnel Department and wrote 'hired' on the form I had given her. When I told

Personnel that I had been offered the job and would start the following week, I was told this was obviously a mistake. I was asked to wait, and had to listen while I heard the phone call expressing concerns about employing a young woman of color. Some months later I came across a memo sent by the editor to the Personnel Department supporting her decision to employ me in the office; this included information about my parents' racial background. I had a sense at the time that I was allowed to continue in this job because of my mother's racial background and therefore I should be given a chance.

The memory of the interview has stayed with me, as a first encounter of discrimination in the workplace, which could have turned out quite differently without confidence to question the process. With the editor's ongoing support and mentorship, this job helped to set me on a path to higher education. She was a middle-class woman, educated at the University of Cambridge, and she introduced me to the world of theater, posh restaurants and good conversation. She arranged for my tuition to be paid at evening classes and I took up her offer to assist me in my educational goals and enrolled in evening classes, completing the necessary qualifications to enter university. We worked together for several years and I became her personal assistant. With her assistance I published my first article during this period about the history of typewriters.

There was some luck involved, as well as the determination to have some kind of career. I wanted to do something with my life, and the thought of working in a telephone factory like my mother motivated me at least to try for something else. This step back into education took some years, beginning with various courses in sociology at a local college to gain a place at university. I was deeply influenced by my experiences in this learning environment; I recollect texts such as *Social Problems of Modern Britain* by Butterworth and Weir (1972) and Worsley (1971) expanding my understanding of sociological theories and perspectives. I warmed to the encouragement of a particular tutor as she showed me how to answer questions in a comprehensive way in preparation for exams. I was still concerned about whether I could make it into university; however, life took a novel turn, when during break time a fellow student (a secretary at the university where I later applied and was accepted to an undergraduate degree course) encouraged me to apply as she observed my engagement and interest in topics in class.

My experiences in higher education are framed by social difference and the feeling of being an 'outsider' searching for some kind of validation in the midst of university culture. The sense of being an 'outsider' in this environment felt complicated because it was filled with excitement, hope, as well as some trepidation. For me, being 'outside' meant I was trying to make my way through a middle-class milieu, miles away from my life experiences. How could I fit in? What were professors speaking about in the large lecture hall? For me, it was an experiment just to see if I could make it through the first year. My thinking was just to go with the flow, taking the nothing ventured, nothing gained approach.

I was fortunate to find new people, some of whom have become lifelong friends, and professors who valued my ideas in meaningful ways. My initial orientation to undergraduate studies and social work took on a passive mode of learning without questioning knowledge presented to me, because of my fear of not knowing whether this form of critique would be well received. I think I felt this more acutely because of my social positioning as a working-class young woman of color. This experience also gave me a feeling of empowered 'difference' in the possibilities of challenge and questioning. Of course, the social context of the time was one in which political (including the unions) and social movements were tied to the opening up of higher education to working-class people.

As a first-generation university student, I felt so enamored to be on the path to a degree. These feelings were clearly linked to my secondary modern school (the equivalent of a high school) experience, where it was clearly understood that working-class girls were destined for factories and, if they were lucky, offices for a few years before marriage and lives as housewives. I remember vividly another layer to this story. In my final school year, I met with a careers advisor who appeared to have no interest in my ambitions and instead told me I would make a good bus conductor on London transport, and continued to give advice on how to apply for this job. This memory has stayed with me and I recoiled inside at the very idea, shifting my thoughts to 'so she thinks because many people of color work as drivers and conductors on the buses, this is my fate – is she saying this because of my racial background?' I had decided long ago that I wanted a career, and I have fond memories of a classmate who wanted to become a teacher; her enthusiasm and determination to pursue this 'middle-class' career, going against the tide of factory work or early marriage, gave me some encouragement. These experiences influenced my first years at university, and so I was driven to understand and articulate as much as I could about theories of Marx, Weber and Popper, amongst others, through reading and attending lectures and seminars.

In retrospect, I am thankful for the Open University texts and their accessible writing style, providing a helpful template for essays and assignments. I entered university at a time when the expansion of higher education opened up opportunities for working-class people to gain an undergraduate degree in the polytechnic era.[4] Throughout the four years of undergraduate studies, radical politics, the civil rights movement in the USA, social class and social policy featured strongly as I recollect this time in my life. My journey through university education resonates with Shields et al. (2011: 65), who comment: 'I sometimes wonder where I would be today without the new language I acquired through the steps of my educational journey.'

When I reflect upon my journey through social work professional training, the use of 'self' was explored using person-centered models to learn ways to communicate and support clients in intellectually and emotionally empathic ways. The Egan model in the text *The Skilled Helper* (1974) was required reading, and in classes these skills were learned through role playing and simulated interviews. Another popular text of the time was the problem-solving text authored by Perlman (1970). These models of direct practice relied upon psychotherapeutic theory orientation, taking a step-by-step process describing each phase of assessment and intervention in problem-solving practice. During this period, social work education largely operated through a psychotherapeutic lens concerned with problems on the individual level rather than making connections with deep structural and social divisions in society. Since the introduction of relationship models in the 1970s, professional thinking about 'the self' has shifted to reflective learning and practice as an integral part of professional development and practice.

My engagement with the 'reflective' process was curtailed in part because I did not recognize its importance and, looking back, I was less responsive to open up my own feelings and thinking about self. At this time, I felt more attuned with the bigger picture of structural barriers and longstanding social divisions of social class, feminism, as well as growing discontent about the unnamed racism of British society. Many students including myself turned to the USA to find literature that addressed issues and concerns of ethnic minority families and communities. One of the important texts that helped filled this void for me and other students in my cohort was Barbara Solomon's *Black Empowerment: Social Work in Oppressed Communities*, published in 1976. Solomon was critical of prevailing models of social work, which seemed to focus on individual failings and adaptation driving structural and social barriers to the periphery. A model of empowerment was proposed drawing together multiple experiences of oppression to develop sets of strategies orientated towards transformation and social change.

The university environment was one in which I sometimes felt constrained in my learning experience because I did not have a sense of being part of (or confidence with) the 'in group.' This marginalized experience was wrapped up with my own working-class background, ethnicity, gender and mixed family background. At that time I felt a sense of displacement (reassuring myself that this was an experiment), as knowledge conveyed in lectures, seminars and other learning circles seemed so distant from my lived experiences, let alone the realities of everyday life. I learned what was expected of me in university cultures and what counts as academic writing and discussion. I used various coping strategies to find a space for my voice in seminars with some professors who encouraged speaking out, and gained solace reading books and articles about feminism and class, supplemented by American civil rights literature expressing hope and possibilities through social change. I often experienced a sense that university was normally a space where only some voices would be listened to or acknowledged through my articulation of social issues which sometimes lacked the presence of students with educational advantage. Some of my frustration was related to the frame of recently arrived and established black communities in academic writing which seemed to focus on 'problems' and the process of assimilation, yet ignore persistent discrimination across housing, employment and in everyday experiences of living. For me these living experiences were further complicated by my family background and my identity. Yet at the same time, I spoke out anyway, attempting to understand more about social problems and how oppressive social conditions in the wider society developed and became entrenched and affected us in personal complex ways. In this context, it is not surprising, then, that reflection seemed like an approach I could do without, lacking the confidence in finding my voice to narrate my lived experiences and engage in this process. I decided it was much better to 'keep my head down' and move through the course; after all, there was so much to learn, work to do and problems to solve. I was unaware of the possibilities of reflective processes for my own personal growth as well as my professional identity.

The empowering experience of discovery and a love of learning through discussions opened up possibilities and transformation as I moved through a course of university study. These memories and reflections framed my thinking and writing, connecting with students' stories of hardship, their families, hopes, privilege, lived experiences, the social conditions of their lives, interests in community activism and capacity building. I discovered the richness of narratives linking personal, practical and theoretical ways of knowing. The meanings in my stories in this section connect me to the past, where I continue to reinterpret stories while living in the present and reforming future stories. What is clear to me now is that in the process of writing, I have been able to begin the study of my own experiences, opening insights into the person I am today in my personal and professional life. This seeking-self project has brought a clearer understanding of reflective practice, its possibilities and pitfalls, connecting with narratives in social work.

Building a global bridge for virtual student exchanges from Los Angeles to London

As social work has become a recognized profession across the world, interest in student exchange programs, international curriculum content, study abroad experiences and faculty collaboration has blossomed. Williams and Graham (2014) note that the 'international' in the social work profession has been developed through these cross-border activities to give social work a global face, to increase knowledge and understanding of human problems. What comes to mind here is that although social work has a shared identity, it is context specific; that is, the conditions in which practice takes place vary between nations, even though many social problems are rooted in international dynamics.

Events such as environmental disasters, war and conflict across the world are brought directly to our attention through various new communication technologies. As Okech and Barner (2014: 169) comment on these factors, 'technology and media have rapidly advanced our ability to recognize places and people across the globe, to see them as facing similar patterns of resource development in the areas of social work services, infrastructure development and issues of discrimination as well as large-scale systemic problems such as environmental concerns, immigration, poverty and political conflict.' In recent years it has become increasingly clear that actions and events in one country may have far-reaching effects across borders, affecting social, economic and political arenas. Confronted with the movement of populations across the world and the need for collaboration to address these issues, international social work is now an established practice field, integrated in the curriculum of most schools of social work. Social work educators have reported that student interest in international social work frequently revolves around wanting to learn more about social problems in different practice contexts, particularly in the areas of policy development and advocacy. In addition, some students are motivated by professional opportunities in international settings, as well as exposure to greater cultural and ethnic diversity (Okech and Barner, 2014).

A net result of these developments has prompted questions about how professional education has responded to international social work. Several organizations such as the International Federation of Social Workers (IFSW) and Association of Schools of Social Work (IASSW) are engaged in global standards for social work as well as setting agendas around contemporary social problems in global contexts. With these issues in mind, my plan in writing this book developed further through a student-to-student exchange project between Dominguez Hills and University of Kingston in Greater London during 2012 and 2013. The project first came to light during an informal meeting in spring 2012 between CSUDH and the University of Kingston, where we discussed what a great idea it would be to link social work students transnationally. We initiated a dialogue about the similarities and differences in the social work profession within respective countries. Having practiced social work for many years in the UK, I am still learning about the breadth of social work practice across agencies and institutions. We discussed using Skype as a platform for the student exchange program as an ongoing international collaborate initiative to provide exposure to international social work practice through student-to-student learning. As field placements offer such important learning experiences, bringing students together from different parts of the world to share experiential learning could provide a unique opportunity to deepen knowledge about the profession (Papouli, 2014). New technologies have opened up opportunities for transnational communications so that many students who are unable to study outside their home country (sometimes because of financial restrictions) or participate in organized student exchange activities can now take advantage of these learning experiences. How do students from different parts of the world perceive and understand social work? What are the realities of practice in different agencies and working environments? In what ways can students build a connection to social work in different social and political contexts? How do these contexts shape welfare arrangements in both countries? Given the significance of social, political and cultural influences in shaping identities and understanding of self, how do these complex processes shape students' practice? What about the difference in educational systems and specifically social work education? These questions helped to shape the following aims and objectives of the project:

- Expand students' experience and understanding of international perspectives in social work.
- Engage critically in understanding the global context of cultural, social and socioeconomic issues in relation to social work practice.
- Enhance the social work education experience of students by providing exposure to international social work practice through building relationships

with students in London with opportunities to share curriculum and ideas about social justice.

- Provide opportunities to discuss a range of conceptual approaches on diversity, including critical race studies and intersectionality (USA), anti-racist and anti-oppressive (UK) and other broader ethical frameworks offered within the USA and UK.
- Allow students to share narratives as they relate to their personal and professional development as social workers.
- Make connections between personal experiences and academic ideas and reflection.
- Explore professional worlds and approaches to practice in different countries.

Setting up the sessions and learning experiences

The student exchange took place on a regular basis for meetings between students at Dominguez Hills in Los Angeles and Kingston University in London over a two-year period. For students at Dominguez Hills it was an early start, with meetings taking place at 8:00 am, and for their counterparts in London it was afternoon meetings at the end of the day. I suspect that our counterparts found meeting after classes at the end of the day or even field placements was particularly challenging in the winter months. Faculty and students were grateful that students in London were committed and enthusiastic about the meetings to engage in dialogue and I also think the street cred of 'Los Angeles' helped things along! After initial introductions and students getting to know one another generally in the respective countries, including why they chose to become a social worker, student-to-student learning took various pathways. Faculty were only present for the first few sessions and then the project continued with students leading the way, covering various topics outlined in the objectives as well as exchanging information and discussions about field placements. This student-led learning project included the exchange of podcasts about students' journeys through social work education, enhancing development of self-awareness intertwined with identities and location of self. Students were asked to identify their social location, gender, age, ethnicity, culture, faith, sexuality, class or any other characteristic that was of significance. Then they shared how they developed their views and outlook about social work practice. The podcasts were shared via SoundCloud and Blackboard, and provided the narrative accounts mentioned earlier.

Next, they considered key aspects of their identities. What values do you hold dear and where do you think they came from? Following on from these questions, how are your values reflected in social work practice? What motivated you to enter the profession of social work? By exchanging fieldwork experiences, differences and similarities in welfare policies, the transnational nature of social problems could be understood in different contexts. This dialogue was framed by exploring social institutions and modes of inequality in respective countries. Personal narratives were an important part of this project, exercised through the creation of podcasts.

Through social work education, students can understand their circumstances through the lens of critical theory and reflection to engage in transformative practice. Posting audio podcasts, students were able to share their personal narratives as, quite often, by hearing another's story, we can develop more insight and understanding of our own. The audio podcasts were available through Blackboard and StudySpace, and accessible to students studying on specific courses.

Some excerpts from students' podcasts

I'm a white, British-born female, in my thirties. My parents are strict Baptists, but I am not practicing. I tend to have a broader sense of my spirituality. I came into social work because, for as long as I can remember, I wanted to help people. As a child, we lived in a very poor neighborhood. But the school I attended was really good. One teacher, in particular, inspired me to dream and to do better. A friend of mine stopped coming to school one day. I really missed her. I later found out that her dad was violent to her and her mum, and that they were moved to a women's refuge. I never saw her again but missed her and often thought of her. When I was at college, I started doing voluntary work with women survivors of domestic abuse. I don't know why, but it's very important to me that everyone – especially the most vulnerable in society – have a voice.

(London, England)

It's been difficult looking at discrimination and oppression on the course – especially as a white person. I realize that there are so many things that I have taken for granted, so many ways I am privileged. Being a woman, especially one who has seen how other women can suffer in violent situations, has made me a bit of a feminist. I have struggled to understand some cultures where I perceive the women to be oppressed, but have learned that they would define themselves differently. I've learned to distinguish between cultural difference and things that may be seen as abusive in any culture. That was quite important for me. So now I check out things, rather than make assumptions.

(London, England)

I will say something about myself. I am white and I come from a working-class background. I am a heterosexual male, 43 years old and have no religious beliefs. Anti-discriminatory practice or, as it is known in America, critical race theory: we have been comparing different social work approaches towards oppression, equality and diversity, and talking about the different ways and issues we face in each of our countries. I began my journey towards social work as a career by qualifying ten years ago as a counselor and counseling in a variety of places, working in the community, mainly counseling lifers in the prison system, and this career led me to work with young people to try and make a difference in their lives at an earlier stage and work with young people in the (state) care system. I worked with young people from 18 up to 25 leaving the care system to help with their transition to adulthood. Many of these young people were emotionally damaged and stigmatized in the community as having problematic behaviors, and it was clear that the trauma they had experienced at an early stage has led to attachment and behavioral issues. I am interested in hearing how these issues are addressed in America and the similar problems social workers face in this location.

(London, England)

I am a black woman, I am heterosexual, middle class, and I am a wife and mother. I have been married for over 12 years and I have three children. The key aspects of my identity is that I am a wife and mother and I hold those dear to me even though I am a full-time student. I still see myself as a stay-at-home mother which is very important to me and my number one role, and this does help shape my value system. The foundation of my values include keeping the family unit as one; a two-parent household for the children so that they can emulate what they see at home; it is a positive environment which is healthy for the children. This is my value set which I hold dear to me. These values came to me through not having a father at home. Growing up without a father has motivated me to become a social worker, as well as the community I was raised in where social workers were seen as baby snatchers; where in real life my mother is a social worker and she encouraged me to become a social worker too.

(Los Angeles, USA)

I am [a] 23-year-old female from Compton. Growing up in Compton has been a very interesting experience – I have lived in Compton all of my life. I have seen the ups and downs of the city, but what made me want to pursue a career in social work is gang violence that exists. My passion is to use education as a tool to help inmates transition into society, but that is difficult because Compton is looked upon as violent and a lot of poverty. And while some of this is true, it doesn't have to stay like that and of course it is difficult because there is reinforcement in songs and videos. I am very happy to be at Dominguez Hills. It is not too far from home and helps me to apply skills locally and look through the lens of critical race theory and the voice of narrative as I am big on allowing others to share their story because only you know yourself better, and to create your own story, allowing the residents of Compton to narrate their own story, not allowing people outside to narrate stories. This is because Compton is not as bad as people may view on the news and elsewhere. This is where my passion lies.

(Los Angeles, USA)

I am male, 26 years old. People here in the United States would identify me as Latino, but I identify myself as an indigenous person coming from a people in southern Mexico where the indigenous population is still very alive – coming from an under-represented community here in Los Angeles – oppression as people looked at us as people who should not persevere and be successful in life – I have overcome many challenges in my life. I am very proud to say that my culture has been influenced by the Catholic religion, even though I don't practice the religion. Growing up, my parents have introduced me to music that we practice in our culture. The traditions and cultural values are being lost year after year as new generations are created, and as part of my social work commitment I would like to help so that groups do not forget about their cultural values as we adapt to the United States. I was taught by my grandparents that the community is for everyone's good, not just for one person's success, but it is about everyone being equal, and it is unfortunate to see where there is discrimination against certain groups as this is not being practiced in society where opportunities are available to some people. Social systems affect how people live on a daily basis so my value is to educate people who have cultural backgrounds in increasing their self-awareness and using some of those traditions that have been lost in making sure equality is integrated in everyone's mind, will and goal. I am all for a multicultural society that has policies in place for all ethnicities, ages and people, and I admire activists who are for that but not radical, and that being said my cultural background brings a tremendous strength and I look forward to having an impact in the local community where I grew up.

(Los Angeles, USA)

I was raised in northern California where my father was a farmer, and through that experience of growing up there I saw the inequalities, the exploitation of labor and a lot of injustice, so a lot of my background and experiences in my life have sparked off wanting to make a difference in people's lives. I have a real passion for helping others and I am currently working as an intern (field placement) at a local college. I am a foster liaison, which means I help foster youth with tutoring and helping them link up with resources, help finding scholarships. I help them register for college and counseling. This has been a very unique experience for me – I have never been exposed to such a diverse group and being part of this university and obtaining my undergraduate [degree] here at Dominguez Hills has helped me a lot. I feel that [the] critical race studies and intersectionality course has helped me understand more and what the field has to offer once I graduate.

(Los Angeles, USA)

I am white – my ethnic background is Swiss, my grandparents came here as immigrants and I was raised as a devout Roman Catholic but have a Jewish father and currently I am a Buddhist, so I have studied many different faiths and have an interesting background. My sexuality is heterosexual and I am a widowed woman, and I was raised in an upper-class family and currently I would say I am middle class. My identity is white and [I] have white privilege, having been raised in the United States which is a racist society. I was also raised by a feminist mother, so I feel I was given that as a gift in society. Feminism in the United States has moved through very different incarnations. We were first considered very radical and then incorporated into the mainstream of society, so feminism has taken a back seat, so often women consider feminism as a step back from progress in some areas, especially myself, if you are a career woman a lot of times your status in society is put on the back burner because you have to choose between either career or family and that is something less prevalent now, but having a feminist mother, she had to choose a career and I think that was difficult for her. I am a documentary filmmaker, which is similar to being a social worker in some regard, as working with the media and looking at injustices of the world and trying to right those injustices through the medium of the visual and audio artistic renderings basically. Documentary filmmaking has evolved in the United States as well now that people have digital cameras; it has become a much more available medium – it used to be a little more exclusive. Still, in the mainstream media it has taken a back seat and to be a documentary filmmaker it is very costly and hard to make a living at that, and this is one of the reasons in my later years to switch to becoming a social worker. I want to go and have a private practice and also work in non-profit organizations to right injustices in the world and to provide services which are not available right now. I am excited about the Affordable Health Act that President Obama has recently signed into law, and hope I can get involved in some way to help implement some the changes in care that are being made in the United States at this time. Being at California State Dominguez Hills has really opened my eyes to critical race studies and I have taken for granted some of the privileges I have in the world; here at Dominguez Hills I am a minority in my class and it has been an interesting juxtaposition, and I feel I have gained a lot of cultural sensitivity being here and I have shifted my orientation as far as looking at the world and looking at other people who haven't had the same opportunities I have had. Thank you.

(Los Angeles, USA)

Thinking about narratives – representing lived experiences

Over the past several decades, narrative has gained interest and popularity across the social sciences and beyond. In the professions, including nursing, law, medicine, occupational therapy and social work, all kinds of narratives have surfaced, from first-person accounts to stories in the field, locating the self in research and descriptions of unfolding events. According to Richardson (2000), 'now narrative is everywhere,' growing in an ever-greater range of areas. Storytelling abounds in movies, books, television, magazines, newspapers and radio, shaping our sense of reality through narratives about people's lives, their experiences and the world in which we live. Narratives are shaped by people's memories of what happened in their past, the stories that are created in their present lives and imagined futures (Richardson, 2000). Our 'life histories' and the way we sequence events into a story are conceived, as McAdams (1993: 11) explains: 'we are all tellers of tales. We seek to provide our scattered and often confusing experiences with a sense of coherence by arranging the episodes in our lives into stories. This is not the stuff of delusion or self-deception. We are not telling ourselves lies. Rather, through our personal myths, each of us discovers what is true and what is meaningful in life.' In this dynamic, narrative gives form to shared beliefs and values on both personal and cultural levels. On the personal level, we have a story of our own lives, which enables us to give meaning to our experiences in constructing who we are and a sense of our futures. Culturally, narratives serve to bring structure to shared beliefs and transmission of values.

The use of narrative in everyday language is closely aligned with storytelling: everyone has a story to tell, gaining strong currency in popular culture. Our interest in the lives of others is a growing trend with the rise of 'reality television' and telling one's story. Here the drama of daily lives has become the main focus of many television programs as people become celebrities and interest in their lives moves beyond these programs and is followed through 'new' media on Facebook, Twitter and YouTube. These forms of media are major producers of narrative, where character, voice and points of view are constructed and directed to produce different kinds of meanings (Fulton, 2006). Life stories followed through forms of media bring myriad experiences in many different social, professional and political contexts. Telling one's story has become a key feature of successful chat shows. For example, the Oprah Winfrey Show took a confessional stance by encouraging people to tell their story because 'the truth will set you free.' This approach generates therapeutic narratives for the camera, drawing audiences into personal accounts, sometimes intertwined with hitherto hidden identities. Now the possibilities of personal transformation come alive from multiple and diverse backgrounds. The term 'narrative turn' has often been used to describe a return to storytelling, with the acknowledgement of its critical importance in life generally for as long as humans have existed. Narratives and storytelling, then, have always had significance in people's lives; they are at the heart of our human reality.

We all love a good story as a way of understanding and being in the world. Narratives bring meaning to our experiences through order by drawing on meaningful connections, attention is paid to identities and the complex way we relate to the world around us and to ourselves. Narratives are often a way of making sense of realities and organizing, interpreting experiences. Like any other social group, professions have their own stories and these narratives are about what they see happening. These stories have become a popular genre; for example, *Call the Midwife* draws audiences to the everyday life of midwives in 1950s east London, where social deprivation and poverty were a familiar sight. The personal lives of the midwives intermingle with their professional nursing duties and relationships with the women and families they serve. The genre of the narrative takes on a personal voice as stories unfold over a lifetime of nursing practice. Storytelling as one aspect of narrative continues to take center stage everywhere, as evidenced in the popularity of StoryCorps and This American Life (National Public Radio), in the way they have inspired many people to share their own personal stories for others to listen to.

Ideas surrounding the term 'narrative' have been taken up in various ways, including social narratives, which are used to describe 'master' stories, some of which are from the distant past yet still have currency and tend to dominate culture in society. As Huisman, amongst others, notes: 'these are stories, or myths, through which a culture tells itself its ideology, its idea of what is natural in its social order' (Huisman, 2006: 16). Many authors have critiqued these stories or myths situated in particular political, economic and social contexts, uncovering the way in which culture is created and transforms social relations and practices through systems of power. Cultural studies as an emerging interdisciplinary field of study responds to a rapidly changing world by articulating the creation of cultural patterns and products in the many facets of popular culture and social practices.

Making connections – reflection and narrative

Self-reflection and narrative are connected, as in making sense of experiences or events a form of agency is created, which takes place with historical, social and cultural contexts. Self-narration is an important way to develop skills of critical reflection through different narrative forms of communication such as poetry, photographs and drawings. I am not alone in thinking about narrative in this way.

Cihodariu (2012: 38) observes: 'being self-aware of one's perceptions and meanings (of one's own narratives …) enriches the depth of understanding in ways some classical investigations cannot.' Learning reflective practice is immediately tied to narratives because this learning process demands listening to a person's story. In this way, theory can be contextualized and assimilated, thus practice can be seen as a series of unfolding narratives (Johns, 2012).

Our identity is key to our being, enabling a sense of self-hood that involves thinking about ourselves in relation to others and the world around us. As social beings, narrative ideas about identity focus on our social character as we became who we are in social contexts as we experience, act, speak and understand the world with others. Identity as storytelling conjures up narratives across the life course. The process is located within social structures and practices in relation to everything around us. This is where the linking of self is tied in with the realities of social existence. In thinking about social conditions, questions arise about how ethnicity, class, gender and other social characteristics shape the stories people tell about themselves. From our experiences in childhood to adulthood and beyond, our identities change with the passing of time in concert with social changes. Understanding the ways in which identity is joined to the social helps to show how stories are shaped in social life. These dynamic processes provide a vehicle for people to make sense of themselves as active meaning makers. As we experience our everyday lives, we become aware of the ways in which social life is littered with language practices or discourses, which shape our thoughts, action and identities as forms of social practice. It is through these systems of meanings that social work is constructed and practiced.

Storytelling, then, is a dynamic process entering the world of a person as they make sense of themselves as an active meaning maker. Narratives are not just personal, they are also cultural, where dominant stories are expressed leaving some narratives and stories on the margins. This allows for the possibility of counter-narratives which contest representations. The use of dialogue has been a key strategy in articulating lived experiences and struggles against oppression.

Reflective stories are maps of our journey, offering insights, unaddressed questions, contradictions, guided by our being and in the present. Vanessa's narrative presents a life story moving through many parts, including evolving identities and emotions bringing strands of lived experiences to weave her account of the social world. These words are not guided by convention; on the contrary, they are awakenings drawing on life as it is lived, understood and felt. Following on, Tejaswini and Michelle's narrative presents a more complicated story about identities and the 'othering' in different locations and contexts. Reflection through narrative as a dialogue with self is clearly present in Frida's narrative, throwing light on its evolving form. Each of the narratives in Part II is never complete and instead unfolding moment to moment, representing a being in place. Johns (2009) considers that we know more about our lives through these conversations in relationship to our surroundings to reveal the storied self as a time to think. In these narratives the reader is invited to dialogue with stories presented to deepen insights as students grapple with evolving identities grounded in 'who am I' as a way of being in practice.

Conclusions

As I review this chapter, I find myself thinking about four themes of personal story, narrative, critical reflection and critical social work. I find myself in the middle of these evolving and interweaving topics, exploring their twists and turns as selected points being taken along through the book. I introduced my story as one of these points of intersection, with teaching and learning from students and their experiences as well as the Skype project opening up transnational explorations about the nature of social work practice in local contexts. With its established origins in literature, history and the humanities, narrative has moved into the social sciences, taking with it creative interpretations of narrative as writing and performance.

Notes

1 Students' accounts in the podcast excerpts have been anonymized.
2 'Prefabs' were modular homes that were built after World War II in the UK because of the housing shortage. The modular homes had a kitchen, living room, two bedrooms and an inside bathroom.
3 Mixed parentage is a term used in the UK. Some readers may be more familiar with biracial.
4 Polytechnics taught both academic and professional vocational degrees, and were originally intended to apply education to work, particularly in engineering and technical subjects.

References

Bold, C. (2012) *Using narrative in research*, London: Sage.

Bolton, G. (2005) *Reflective practice, writing and professional development* (2nd edn), London: Sage.

Butterworth, E. and Weir, D. (1972) *Social problems of modern Britain*, London: Fontana Press.

Cihodariu, M. (2012) 'Narratives as instrumental research and as attempts of fixing meaning the uses and misuses of the concept "narratives",' *Journal of Comparative Research in Anthropology and Sociology*, 3(2): 27–43.

Clough, P. (2002) *Narratives and fictions in educational research*, Buckingham: Open University.

Clutterbuck, D.A. (2001) *Everyone needs a mentor: fostering talent at work* (3rd edn), London: CIPD.

Cooper, L. (2006) 'Mirror, mirror on the wall, who is the fairest of all?,' *Journal of Practice Teaching and Learning*, 7(1): 22–38.

Cree, V.E. (2013) *Becoming a social worker: global narratives* (2nd edn), London: Routledge.

Danto, E. (2008) 'Some words, different meanings: notes toward a typology of postmodern social work education,' *Social Work Education*, 27(7): 710–722.

Egan, G. (1974) *The skilled helper: a model for systematic helping and interpersonal relating*, Monterey, CA: Brooks/Cole.

Ellis, C. (1993) 'There are survivors: telling a story of sudden death,' *The Sociological Quarterly*, 34(4): 711–730.

Ellis, C. (2004) *The ethnographic I: a methodological novel about auto ethnography*, Walnut Creek, CA: Alta Mira Press.

Ellis, C. and Bochner, A.P. (1999) 'Bringing emotion and personal narrative into medical social science,' *Health*, 3(2): 229–237.

Fook, J. (2012) 'The challenges of creating critically reflective groups,' *Social Work with Groups*, 35: 218–234.

Fulton, H. (2006) 'Introduction: the power of narrative.' In H. Fulton, *Narrative and Media*, New York: Cambridge University Press, pp. 1–11.

Graham, M. and Schiele, J. (2010) 'Anti-discriminatory and equality of oppressions models in social work: reflections from the UK and USA,' *European Journal of Social Work*, 13(2): 231–244.

Healy, K. and Leonard, P. (2000) 'Responding to uncertainty: critical social work education in the postmodern habitat,' *Journal of Progressive Human Services*, 11(1): 23–48.

Herrmann, A. and DiFate, K. (2014) 'Introduction to the special issue: the new ethnography: Goodall, Trujillo and the necessity of storytelling,' *Storytelling, Self, Society*, 10(1): 299–306.

Huisman, R. (2006) 'Narrative concepts.' In H. Fulton (ed.), *Narrative and media*, Cambridge: Cambridge University Press, pp. 11–28.

Hyvarinen, M. (2008) 'Analyzing narratives and story-telling.' In P. Alasuutari, L. Bickman and J. Brannen (eds), *The Sage handbook of social research methods*, London: Sage, pp. 447–461.

Johns, C. (2009) *Engaging reflection in practice, a narrative approach*, Oxford: Blackwell.

Johns, C. (2010) *Guided reflection: a narrative approach to advancing professional practice*, Oxford: Wiley.

Johns, C. (2012) 'How holistic are we? The role of narrative, storytelling and reflection in the development of holistic practice,' *European Journal of Cancer Care*, 21: 561–564.

Lyons, N. (2010) *Handbook of reflection and reflective inquiry*, New York: Springer.

McAdams, D. (1993) *The stories we live by: personal myths and the making of self*, New York: W. Morrow.

Morley, C. (2008) 'Teaching critical practice: resisting structural domination through critical reflection,' *Social Work Education*, 27(4): 407–421.

Okech, D. and Barner, J. (2014) 'Students' motivations for taking an international social work elective course,' *Journal of Teaching in Social Work*, 34(2): 167–181.

Papouli, E. (2014) 'Field learning in social work education: implications for educators and instructors,' *The Field Educator Journal*, Simmons School of Social Work, 4(2): 1–15.

Perlman, H.H. (1970) 'The problem-solving model in social casework.' In R.W. Roberts and R.H. Nee (eds), *Theories of social casework*, Chicago: The University of Chicago Press, pp. 131–179.

Polkinghorne, D. (1988) *Narrative knowing and the human sciences*, Albany: State University of New York Press.

Richardson, B. (2000) 'Recent concepts of narrative and the narratives of narrative theory,' *Style*, 34(2): 168–175.

Schön, D. (1991) *The reflective practitioner*, Aldershot: Ashgate.

Shields, C., Novak, N., Marshall, B. and Guiney Yallop, J. (2011) 'Providing visions of a different life: self-study narrative inquiry as an instrument for seeing ourselves in previously-unimagined places,' *Narrative Works, Issues, Investigations and Interventions*, 1(1): 63–77.

Solomon, B. (1976) *Black empowerment: social work in oppressed communities*, New York: Columbia University Press.

Vertovec, S. (2008) 'Superdiversity and its implications,' *Ethnic and Racial Studies*, 30(6): 1024–1054.

West, L. (1996) *Beyond fragmentation: adults, motivation and higher education*, London: Routledge.

Williams, C. and Graham, M. (2014) '"A world on the move": migration, mobilities and social work,' *British Journal of Social Work*, 44 (Supplement 1): i1–i17.

Worsley, P. (1971) *Problems in modern society*, Harmondsworth: Penguin.

2

REFLECTIVE LEARNING TO CRITICAL REFLECTION

Models and background stories

Introduction

Social workers spend lots of time listening to client stories to understand their circumstances and to get a sense of the difficulties they are experiencing. These stories are then repeated in assessment and considered in planning interventions and advocating for their needs. In the midst of the realities of practice, awareness of our own thoughts, feelings and attitudes in relationships with clients are often given short shrift. Yet our feelings are important as they affect our ability to understand our experiences. It is generally agreed that becoming a reflective practitioner requires a range of skills, including thinking, learning and assessment of self for reflection and action. This process helps social workers to find ways to understand professional issues for themselves. In identifying who we are, our subjective thoughts, how we see and act in the world, we are able to build capacity in acknowledging the complexity and uncertainty in present-day social work practice.

Before moving on to developments in reflective inquiry, it is useful at this point to be reminded about learning in practice from both the classroom (theory) and field settings (practice knowledge) necessary to become a professional social worker. As a practice-based profession, the strategies of reflection have been described as key to developing a professional self. Reflective approaches allow students to explore the complexities of values, emotions or relationships. Ingram et al. (2014) point out that reflective practice is the only way to think through properly the array of tensions while adhering to values embedded in the profession. In crafting a platform for practice, there are different kinds of learning, both formal and informal, which are sometimes intertwined and drawing a clear distinction between them can be difficult, particularly when the goal of integration in both classroom and field is embedded in social work education. Generally speaking, formal learning (explicit knowledge) tends to be highly structured and usually connected with academic classroom-based learning. When it comes to informal learning, this often takes place in practice settings, is self-directed, experiential and linked to daily experiences (Papouli, 2014).

For many decades, reflective practice has been a key learning strategy in the development of professional education. As professions developed in higher education, new colleges were created to educate students in specialized knowledge alongside a set of obligations and values often expressed in a professional code of ethics. In short, these features shaped professional commitments to protect people from harm, accountability and offer guidance for practitioners. The main thrust of professional education consists of bringing together theoretical knowledge through a framework of values and skills on the practice front. This process proved to be tricky not least because professional training relies upon gaining knowledge and theory, which is later translated into practice. How does the application of knowledge to professional practice work? What are the ins and outs of this process, and more specifically how can application translate and support competent practice? The phrase 'practice makes perfect' is often used to describe the value of experiential learning in professional development.

Confronted with unease and skepticism around the gap between theories taught in classrooms and day-to-day practice, Schön (1983) asked searching questions, including how do professionals operate in practice and how do they know what they know? Not surprisingly, these questions revealed several shortcomings about the realities of practice on the ground. Schön (1983) wrote a widely quoted text, *The Reflective Practitioner*, proposing a new way of thinking about professional practice to address discrepancies arising from what professionals say they do and what actually happens on the practice floor. Surveys among professionals, set up by Argyris and Schön (1974), confirmed the mismatch between theory and practice. Schön describes this contrast in the following way: 'On the high ground, manageable problems lend themselves to solution through application of research-based theory and technique. In the swampy lowland, messy, confusing problems defy technical solution' (Schön, 1987: 3).

The reasons for this implementation gap are many, ranging from organizational to cultural factors as well as unconscious decisions masking practitioners' insight. Perhaps the most significant developments arising from this identifiable gap between professional aspirations and the realities of practice are models of reflective practice filled with their own interpretations and uses of reflection (Murphy et al., 2010). The widespread adaptation of reflective practice as a way of developing professionalism has led to formal assessments by regulatory bodies including the need for individual students to demonstrate reflective practice. Before I turn to reviewing models of reflection in social work practice, the next section briefly gives an account of trends in social work approaches and methods, all of which are relevant to this chapter.

The background of reflective practice in social work can be found in its psychotherapeutic origins, where the understanding and the use of self formed an essential characteristic of professional practice. There is a longstanding tradition of casework in social work drawing upon a psychodynamic and psychology knowledge base. As Rogowski (2010: 48) observes, 'this being a focus for professionalization and legitimating its location in the "psy" complex. Its distinctive contribution was the claim that it was concerned with the whole person, and with providing person skills in human relationships and an understanding of individuals and families.'

Casework in the 1960s continued to place great emphasis on individual pathology as central to treatment and change. Lavalette (2011), amongst others, refers to the way structural disadvantage was hardly recognized in casework during this time and often failed to meet the needs of these communities. Living conditions and life chances influenced by social class, ethnicity and other social divisions received little attention in social work education. Practitioners were trained to pay more attention on individual problems and treatment approaches, often leaving out other family members let alone other systems of support. The concern here is that these approaches relied exclusively on psychological explanations.

Over time, it was generally agreed that more integrated approaches were needed to take into account social disadvantage linked to poverty, unemployment and housing needs of clients. In light of these concerns and connections to broader political and social contexts, interest in sociological perspectives to understand social problems came into view. By the 1990s, greater scrutiny of casework and psychodynamic approaches inspired a broader repertoire of practice interventions within sociopolitical and cultural contexts. In an important sense, casework with its clinical orientation was eclipsed by social justice ambitions situated in the wider society as the core mission of the profession. Tensions between macro- and micro-approaches to social work education began to surface and the critique of reflection based upon its 'psychologism' and its association with clinical practice (Knott, 2007; Murphy et al., 2010; Urdang, 2010).

Another general point to make is that in British and US professional education generally, models of reflection took hold as a core element in actively engaging learners with theory in practice (Ixer, 2010). It is also worth noting here several other changes that cut across emerging trends within the profession – back stories, so to speak, affecting the position of reflective practice in social work. High-profile cases of child deaths intensified loss of confidence in professional expertise raising questions about the shortcomings of social work and the need to regulate and identify good practice. These concerns are closely aligned to a move towards systems of accountability. In this context, competency-based learning was introduced as a measure of assessment with its focus on defined tasks and performance indicators rather than process as a holistic approach to practice. Competency is referred to as 'being able to demonstrate knowledge, values and skills learned can be integrated into practice' (Damron-Rodriguez, 2008: 30). While this emphasis on assessment of competence and what works directed through frameworks of requirements has had a powerful influence on social work education, critical arguments have come to light citing this bureaucratic approach to practice as 'description and prescription' which ignores the potential for professional judgment and has no regard for influence of social context or settings.

In understanding this trend, competency-driven approaches underpin a shift away from a concern about people and relationship building (Cooper and Broadfoot, 2006). In the grip of the drive to codify practice, Gould and Taylor (1996) point to weaknesses of competency-driven methods which lie in a largely functionalist underpinning often leading to the checkbox approach measured against a template of learning tasks. Several authors have called for the self in professional social work to be rehabilitated in a postmodern context embracing partnerships with clients or service users. Similar developments have taken place with the introduction of evidence-based practice which relies on technical/rational knowledge and a top-down approach in its application (Schön, 1983; Murphy et al., 2010; Urdang, 2010).

In thinking about reflective practice, several commentators have debated its place in social work practice, arguing that there is no such thing as reflection (Ixer, 1999). Ixer (1999) believes since there is no clear definition of reflection, our understanding about the concept is inadequate. Taking this point further, he raises questions about the soundness of assessing reflective practice as a measured outcome in professional development. Ixer observes: 'such is the underdevelopment of reflective methodology in general that there is little evidence of reflection training of any kind in the social work curriculum. Furthermore, we simply do not have the assessment tools to measure what students are doing when they are reflecting' (Ixer, 1999: 520). While he adds 'reflective learning has come to enjoy a cult following amongst curriculum planners and those responsible for professional education,' others point to the central role of reflective learning in professional development (Ixer, 1999: 513). In support of reflective practice in social work, Murphy et al. (2010: 176) suggest the exciting possibilities of reflective practice, pointing to opportunities to assist practitioners to move from practice to theory by extracting and articulating theory and knowledge embedded in their practice.

It would be remiss of me at this point not to acknowledge the different terms and explanations surrounding the complex process of reflection. It should be apparent by now that reflection is a process of thinking about an issue or situation embedded in experience. Through the frame of interpretative discovery, differences emerge in the process from the multiple meanings of reflection from ideas of introspection to critical dialogue. As these connections between the process of learning through experience and evaluating own responses to practice situations are subject to various interpretations and understandings, some educators and practitioners prefer one interpretation rather than another. However, the question often asked is what is reflection? A straightforward answer would be understanding the feelings experienced by self and others. Yet this response lacks the description and deeper understanding played out in expanded models of reflection, which include critical reflection, reflection in action and reflexivity, all of which describe different elements and processes.

Johns (2009) helpfully summarizes key points in thinking about reflection and reflective practice:

- Reflection is shaped by ideas of being in the world rather than doing.
- The quality of reflective practice is found in the lived experience and becoming mindful of self rather than just learning through experience.
- The act of reflection is an experience in and of itself.
- The insights of reflection can offer people more satisfactory and fulfilling lives.
- From a holistic perspective, reflective practice requires energy work in nurturing commitment, dissipating anxiety, finding meaning, becoming vision, realizing power, knowing self.

Reflection and critical thinking

When we think about reflection, what comes to mind is a process of examining a range of experiences and factors in decisions or situations taking place in practice. Being reflective involves self-awareness and the process of thinking through sometimes complicated situations in a holistic way. This grounding in practice also draws on understanding one's own values, assumptions and constructions of meaning, resilience and openness to possibilities and hope.

Although much has been written about being reflective, often with a focus on the nuts and bolts of 'reflection' as a kind of thinking, in recent times 'critical thinking' has been integrated into this framework bringing ideas about conscious interrogation of the social, cultural and political contexts of society. These qualities are often bandied about as if somehow these important skills will pop out after several lectures, seminars and writing assignments. Rather than expecting a quick fix, to start this journey Bolton (2005) invites us to critically reassess ourselves, our ideas, our values and assumptions to develop human understanding through identity and sense of self and lived experiences.

Fook (2002: 38) encourages an awareness of how our own theories and understandings about the social world are translated into practice. She writes: 'the reflective approach recognizes that theory is often implicit in the way professionals act and may or may not be congruent with the theory they believe themselves to be acting upon ... reflexivity takes this further, drawing attention to the perspective of the knower' and 'encourages use to explore other perspectives ... to try on the perspective, the world view of an "other" for long enough to look back critically at ourselves, our ideas, our assumptions, our values.' In a nutshell, critical reflection serves to facilitate the challenge of looking back over events with a critical eye to our underlying beliefs, values and assumptions to question accepted truths and to consider alternative interpretations.

Reflection in action

From reflection to critical reflection skips over other kinds of reflective processes evolving over time. One such process is reflection in action, when professionals think about what they are doing while they are doing it. In other words, reflection takes place in practice, offering more than just adapting, adjusting and responding to what has already taken place. Rather, reflecting all the time, crafting through practice partly at an unconscious level to get through the experience. Skills in reflecting in this way do not come overnight but rather with years of experience. This is where crafting practice wisdom to bear as reflection takes place throughout the process. Practitioners rarely have time to think about reflection in this objective way, yet this level of reflection incorporates not only what has been learned but how it may help the current situation.

Reflexivity

On a basic level reflexivity is another way of thinking about reflection in action which occurs in the midst of practice. In this context, reflexivity draws practice back on itself so that we can utilize present experiences to 'think the problem out' and improve ongoing practice. This involves introspection in the moment in the act of looking back and this reflection on practice becomes the object of scrutiny. Payne (2002) explains reflexivity as a circular process in which our actions may need to change according to evidence we see about the effect we are having. It is generally acknowledged that the most significant reflection is one which is self-motivated because here the person is following their own agenda in trying to make sense of their own learning and wants to make things better.

Let's look at models of reflection

It is apparent by now that as social work is a practice-based profession, reflective thinking is a strong element in maintaining a professional identity. Much has been written about reflection over the past decade, in many different ways and various forms. With all these discussions about reflective practice, it would be easy to give the impression that the reflective approach is an alternative to taking theory into practice. Learning from practice and taking this knowledge without any reference to theory or research fails to acknowledge the significance of professional knowledge in social work (Thompson and Thompson, 2008). There is no doubt that some form of reflection and skills associated with this process is a key function of education and professional practice. However, as Gardner (2014) points out, critical reflection has much to offer in all aspects of personal as well as professional life in offering a way to more deeply understand our reactions to everyday life challenges and possibilities. For this author, this kind of reflection is an attitude to life in general and tied to personal development in a holistic way.

A number of useful models for reflection have been developed over the years. The work of Schön (1983) has been particularly influential in developing a model of reflective practice in professional training and education. Taking as his main focus concerns about the relationship between theory and practice, he articulates the need to pay closer attention to the discrepancy between the ideal (theory) and the real world on the practice floor to find out what professionals actually do in practice. He wanted to delve deeper into finding more about knowledge valued in the academy and whether this knowledge can be directly applied to practice. Schön articulated his skepticism about this process and went on to describe this traditional approach as 'technical rationality' (a particular view of knowledge), which does not match the messy and often confusing problems in practice. Central to this critique of technical approaches to professional practice is its reliance on mechanical, fixed ways of working in finding the right answers on how to proceed. The origins of this approach can be found 'in the late nineteenth century when positivism was at its height, and the professional schools which secured their place in the university in the early decades of the twentieth century' (Schön, 1983: 31).

What stands out in Schön's writing is his assertion that professionals can exhibit a kind of knowing through practice. He suggests this kind of knowing is sometimes difficult to convey because often practitioners know more than they can say. This knowledge is found in the experience they use to develop more effective action strategies. In other words, practitioners have to think on their feet and in doing so have to think about what they are doing while they are in the midst of action. It is a 'dialogue of thinking and doing through which I become more skillful' (Schön, 1987: 31). He maintained that this view of knowledge in practice can be viewed in two ways as separate activities, as knowing in action and reflection on action.

Using this framework of active problem solving, the development of knowledge in action is at the core of reflective practice. This elaboration of experiential knowledge is based upon prior understandings, asking questions such as 'how am I framing this problem?' and engaging with open thinking and awareness of the many faces of reality. In addition, professionals should step back and reflect upon their own professional action and learning from their experiences. Schön likened the reflective practitioner to an artist who is able to capture the world in different ways, crafting appropriate solutions to fit a specific practice situation. Bager-Charleson (2010: 39) describes this process as involving 'an openness to the suggestion that life can look different depending on where you try to "capture" it. However, even if you are artistic and bring materials into the room with which to work creatively, the ultimate work should not rely upon sharpened pencils but on you – you bring only yourself as a tool.'

By making meaningful links between knowledge and practice, the practitioner can harness practice experiences to shape professional growth actively. Schön's insights are significant to understanding reflective practice, bringing the integration of experience and learning together as a process of knowledge advancing and improving professional practice. Schön (1983), who has written extensively on many aspects of reflection, views the capacity to reflect as a continuous process of learning, and in many ways this manner of thinking is grounded in projects of health, well-being and lifelong learning. Of course, people prefer different kinds of reflection and these preferences take place across different levels and at particular times during life journeys. In social work contexts, reflection is tied to the general idea of professionalism with a view to improving practice through learning from experience. In this sense, reflection is a skill developed in moving from a novice to an expert with the ability to get things done almost as second nature with an intuitive grasp of the situation with a clear understanding of what should happen next. Apart from getting things done, the process of questioning and reflecting enables the expert to grow and share reflections with other professionals. In understanding reflection, it is important to note that reflection is more than looking backwards or thinking as navel gazing about our experiences. Instead this process intrinsically captures a form of dialogue explained as 'an engagement that is ongoing ... as opposed to a single, monetary encounter. In the process of trying to understand the other, our own beliefs and assumptions are disclosed, and these assumptions, themselves, can become objects of examination and critique' (Bager-Charleson, 2010: 15).

Helpful aspects of Schön's approach

In summary, what are the key contributions made by Schön's approach to reflective practice?

- Schön's (1983) perspective revealed the need to move beyond the limits of technical knowledge to embrace a framework for practice-based theory.
- He showed through the use of reflection that conflicting views in the different worlds of practice can be reconciled.
- He identified the artistry of practice.
- It was an embodied type of reflection through knowing in action in professional practice.

Professional values

Social work has often been described as a valued-based profession keeping a set of standards about how social workers should behave with clients. These values are respect for human worth and dignity, client self-determination and confidentiality, non-judgmental attitude, controlled emotional involvement and belief in capacity for change (Biestek, 1961). This list approach has been taken up by many professional associations in their codes of ethics, for example the National Association of Social Workers (NASW, 1996) in the USA, the Australian Association of Social Workers (AASW), the British Association of Social Workers (BASW) and the International Federation of Social Workers (IFSW) in 1994. Of late, social work values in the form of listings have been extensively criticized, not least because there is often little explanation surrounding the complexity, interpretations and conflicts between these prescribed 'simply' pictured preferences in real life practice situations. In working with values, Walmsley and Birbeck (2006: 113) recognize 'values emerge from lived experience – through interaction and social exchanges in families, communities, cultures, and societies.' Here, there is a clear link with our own personal narratives and reflective practice, and in these ways each practitioner is constituted within a social context bringing to the practice floor a lens with which to view the social world (Walmsley and Birbeck, 2006). In other words, we bring all aspects of ourselves to the social processes of value construction, including power relations implicated in societal stories and narratives. A further issue widely discussed is that values adopted by the profession are based largely on values embedded in Western societies. All these developments have led to a more comprehensive and nuanced understanding of values in practice situations. Getting to grips with the many debates and discussions about ethics and values can be a tricky enterprise; however, there is no doubt that values have helped greatly to ensure a good starting point for reflective practice.

Postmodernism, critical theory and reflective practice

Looking at the influential texts from the 1970s, models of reflection based upon casework and psychodynamic approaches lacked consideration of broader social, economic and political contexts. The introduction of a range of theoretical approaches challenged exclusive relationship-based models at the core of social work practice. As outlined earlier, reflective practice originated to address problems in professional practice with a focus on internal thought processes with little recognition of context, power dynamics or ideological challenge (Bradbury et al., 2010). On top of these developments, Parton (2002), amongst others, recognized that the social work profession, embedded as it is in social and political contexts, has experienced a major period of social change implicated in day-to-day practice and organization, unsettling longstanding theories and established knowledge creating uncertainty on the practice front. These challenges have sparked debate about not only the nature and direction of social work, but also how to develop and integrate new approaches into everyday practice. Walker (2001: 35) poses the question: 'if the profession is to embrace a postmodernist perspective and subject all theory and practice to critical analysis and deconstruction [how can we have] confidence in any set of intellectual skills'?

A starting point for this section is to map out postmodern approaches in a general way. Moving on, I want to give an example of the influence of postmodern knowledge across the social sciences by highlighting new insights in revised understandings of the body and its connections with social work practice. Postmodern insights into the construction of knowledge and social work practice have become significant in recent years not least because it is well recognized that sociology and psychology are the main building blocks for social work.

Postmodern theories are at the heart of understanding and thinking about our experiences in the social world. Postmodern perspectives have something to say about the ways in which societies are changing, leading to a rethink about social arrangements in everyday life which are not fully accounted for by earlier approaches. This shift has turned away from abstract macro-sociological problems toward the everyday characteristics of modern social living. The sociology of everyday life has paved the way for analysis across the qualities and micro-context of modern social life bringing new perspectives on love, intimacy, friendship, shopping, being single, GPS and mobile phones, health and fitness, life documents as records of experience and life stories (Sztompkai, 2008).

Another example of postmodern exploration is the social and cultural under-standings of the body in social and political contexts across interdisciplinary fields. With connections linked to health concerns, our bodies are the center of consumer culture, filled with goods and programs to make us look and feel healthy and youthful. The interrogation of these socio-cultural platforms has uncovered more about our relationships with our bodies as well as management of the body project through narratives claiming 'truths' operating across multi-dimensional spaces in society. Of course, the body is central to everyday practice, as social workers are often working with people who have been influenced by painful, traumatic or demeaning experiences. Interestingly, it is the wave of postmodern insights that have brought bodies back into social work practice, revealing meanings ascribed to bodies and new understandings of embodied experiences in the wider society (Tangenberg and Kemp, 2002). In thinking about the body and social work practice, Tangenberg and Kemp provide three potent areas of interest. First, the way we experience our bodies in everyday life. It is through our bodies that we make sense of the world; although it may sound obvious, our bodily experiences are important to our well-being. The effects of illness and our experiences become heightened in this context. After asking the question of how social work can validate and value lived experiences, Tangenberg and Kemp (2002) offer narratives as a way for people to speak to their bodily experiences.

Second, the body of power: this is the physicality of oppression and marginality through external marking of the body although socially constructed race, ethnicity, age, gender and disability and sexual orientation can signify social location. According to postmodern thinking, power is varied, dispersed and can be exercised in many different forms. Bodies are ascribed with perceived power based on ethnicity, race, age, gender, disability and sexual orientation. Workings of power influence relationships between bodies, their experiences and social institutions.

Third, the client body is understood through the way in which 'people become clients, their bodies and bodily experiences are named, classified, and organized according to the services they receive' (Tangenberg and Kemp, 2002: 15). Social institutions, such as social work, are implicated in shaping perceptions of identity in many areas of practice, for example, a mental health diagnosis can direct people's lives in many ways, so their mental health diagnosis becomes the person they are rather than a person first with mental health difficulties. New ways of thinking about mental health have surfaced as user movements have pushed through recovery models to dampen and revise traditional medical models used by social work practitioners. There are other examples of professional knowledge and expertise having unintended consequences and leading to reinforcing stereotypes in wider society. In the main, social work has been reliant on objective knowledge in modes of treatment, which sometimes belittles or ignores embodied knowledge of people receiving services. These concerns bring us back to the importance of power implicated in the creation of knowledge and what knowledge is valued and per-ceived as acceptable in professional circles. Postmodern trends have created spaces to examine social life and institutions in different ways to reveal the way in which the voices with least social power can be heard. Bringing the body into social work has enriched our practice as demographic shifts and trends adopting well-being models of health require new understanding of embodied experiences and the meanings ascribed to bodies in the wider society.

As social change has become a common feature in everyday life, many commentators have suggested these changes cannot be explained by traditional theories about class, race, gender and socialization that seemed to work in previous eras. It is often argued that traditional boundaries between social groups are breaking down and it is more difficult currently in society to predict the lifestyles that people will adopt. Postmodern themes critique reliance on grand theories because they tended to present a general theory of differences between social groups. For example, feminist theories seemed to present women as a homogenous group with similar experiences and little emphasis upon the differences between women – say for example, women of color – and gendered experiences of oppression.

As postmodern perspectives embrace local narratives – that is, differences between people and social groups rather than similarities – highlighting local circumstances and individual experiences is important in shaping identities. Some of these issues and experiences are explored in Tejaswini's narrative as she moves from India to Australia and speaks about her new identity as an ethnic and religious minority. These complications are closely connected with 'othering' and meanings in different ways and geographical locations. In reading Tejaswini's narrative in the second section of this book, she wrestles with the ambiguity and complexity of these concerns, offering a first-person practice story. On another level, in the past, political activism through social movements was based on theories that attempted to explain things on a larger scale. These 'big' stories served a useful purpose in leading projects of emancipation towards social change. With these powerful critiques, it has been difficult to sustain collective narratives inherent in social movements of the past. Rapid social change has deflated these trends, leading to new ways of generating campaigns and protest through forms of social media and beyond. In this era, multiple identities – for example, gender, race and disability – in a frame of interconnections (intersectionality) are given prominence together with experiences of living in understanding the individual, their identity and conditions of social life. Notions of a single identity are replaced with alternative emphasis on 'identities' reflecting individuals' socially available choices which change and evolve according to situations and social contexts as a never-ending project through the life course. Identities are created, imposed and can be repressed by social institutions and interactions, and at the same time they are fragmented and multidimensional. The self as a complex web of intersectional identities provides a more nuanced understanding of individuals and social relations in society (Graham and Schiele, 2010). The term intersectionality has emerged over the past decade as a way of studying the intersection of social categories which contribute to experiences of both oppression and privilege. This orientation reveals different types of discrimination that can occur within these intersections in assessing their impact on converging identities.

Postmodern perspectives have clearly unsettled dominant explanations about social divisions that underpin anti-oppressive practice and thinking about social life. Some commentators have bemoaned its undermining of collective histories of hitherto marginalized groups and their struggles to have their voices heard (Dominelli, 2007). If we accept this worldview, then postmodern perspectives have opened up other lines of inquiry, some of which support critical perspectives including narrative, experiential knowledge, biographical research, auto-ethnography and life histories. Confronted with the notions of diffuse rather than concentrated power according to social context and situations, power relations are framed by changing complexities of contemporary life. Bearing in mind these new directions, Merrill and West (2009: 29) share these individualized approaches in the collective sense: 'women's stories high-lighted their oppression in society but also provided a means to transform women's lives, illustrating how individual problems are also collective ones … the personal, direct experience, underlies all behaviours and actions. The influence of these ideas was to find expression in research with other and diverse marginalized groups.'

By introducing the world of the social as socially constructed, then, post-modernism calls into question conventional ideas about knowledge as neutral and objective to untangle its connections with power. From this perspective there are no universal 'truths' because there are multiple ways of knowing, recognizing different points of view are equally valid. As knowledge is socially constructed, the links between knowledge and power are critical to understand its power dynamics tied to specific historical and social contexts. Payne (2014: 18) explains social constructionism as 'what we call reality is social knowledge that has been agreed between people because having a shared view about how things work between people helps us to live an ordered life … However, we all have slightly different views of that social reality, because we all see and interpret what happens around us in slightly different ways, and this varies according to our life experience.'

There are many ways in which postmodern thinking has influenced social sciences, mostly shedding light on the micro-level making connections to wider social structures and operations of power. A great deal of attention in this frame-work is given to language as generating what we experience as realities. As Brown and Augusta-Scott (2007: xx) point out, 'meaning does not already exist, but comes into being through the use of language.' This view of language examines its use and structure and how its expression shapes knowledge production. The recognition of language as a driver shapes understanding about how we construct our world and appreciate locally experienced realities. The term 'discourse' is often used to describe 'the ways in which we make meaning of and construct our world through the language we use (verbal and non-verbal) to communicate about it' (Fook, 2002: 63). Discourses are important in society because they contain sets of meanings, some of which become dominant and others are excluded. In this way, we can see the way in which power differences operate to sustain dominant social realities embedded in cultural, as well as social, political and professional contexts. These linkages bring to light a new politics of knowledge and power as inseparable and joined through discourse (Foucault, 1972). Postmodern inquiry deconstructs these discourses to uncover social meanings and take for granted assumptions that frame our thinking in different ways. Combs and Freedman (2012: 1038) provide a helpful way of describing modern power:

> modern power, instead of coming from a central authority, is carried in discourses. Through lobbying, advertising, participating on school boards, and a thousand other means, the more privileged people in a society have more influence on its discourses. We do not usually notice the powerful influence of these discourses … modern power recruits us into policing ourselves … once we learn to look for the workings of power, we can question its influence.

At this point, this discussion about theoretical perspectives may seem a million miles away from the practice front. How can this way of thinking about knowledge be linked in a way that extends to the practice floor in a meaningful way? Postmodern thinking not only helps us in dealing with the complexity and multiple contexts in which practice takes place but also helps us to appreciate that knowledge in practice is not a one-way process but rather a relationship that is shaped by knowledge both professional and client led. Current work in narrative practice and therapy harnesses these ideas to craft an approach (see Epston and White, 1992) in which people's problem stories are changed through immersing themselves in their life stories that offer different possibilities and directions, placing people as the experts in their own lives. By focusing on meanings, externalizing problems and re-authoring conversations, this framework has created a bottom-up method integrating complex postmodern theories into practice (Beres, 2014). There are other ways postmodern thinking has framed social work methods and practice, but perhaps narrative practice has developed well-thought-out approaches.

Practitioners can continue to draw on the breadth of postmodern approaches to help understand the challenges they face in engaging constructively with dilemmas and issues that arise in professional practice (Gardner, 2014). At this point it is helpful to highlight some of the main themes of postmodern theory and critique in crafting contours of practice.

- Multiple ways of knowing – recognizing different points of view as equally valid.
- Knowledge is socially constructed and best understood as a form of power that is linked to specific historical and social contexts.
- Critique of methods of practice based upon universal formulas.
- Critique of essentialism is replaced by a nuanced focus on fluid, dynamic and changing identities, cultures, diversity and difference.
- Meanings and realities are constructed out of language and they should be explained in relation to historical, political and social contexts.
- Practice guidance instead of practice prescription.
- Recognition of complexities of power relationships, leaving behind ideas of power as possessed but rather exercised in different ways and situations.

- Fragmented view of collective experiences and histories.
- Multi-dimensional aspects of identity.

I will return to postmodern connections between knowledge and power more fully in the context of research and narrative in the next chapter.

Postmodern encounters with social work, reflection and critical theory

Initially social work was generally reluctant to take postmodern perspectives into its knowledge base because it seemed to 'upset the apple cart' by challenging many assumptions in the way we see problems in the field of practice and questions about the profession itself. Postmodernism may seem interesting in a personal way; however, its critique of the profession and deconstruction (taking apart and examination) lays bare troubling issues driving revised thinking about central principles in social work (Danto, 2008). Nonetheless, as postmodern influences spread into the professions generally, these challenges could no longer be ignored. Subsequently, postmodernism has slowly crept its way into social work knowledge and practice, bringing about revised frameworks of knowledge and crafting different forms of practice which suggest that social workers have to adapt to ongoing changing conditions. Postmodern analysis has brought about scrutiny of social work itself, its professional culture and disciplinary role in day-to-day practice. One particular area of interest has been the need to revise and invigorate critical approaches to social work. Earlier in this chapter, I discussed the changes in orientations shaping social work practice, from exclusively psychodynamic and individualized theory and practice to the development of more integrated approaches addressing wider social and political issues.

Critical traditions in social work have been at the core of social work since its inception, with a common focus on social justice and social reform. The term 'critical' in reflective practice has been used across many different disciplines and critical has many variations in its meanings and application in reflection. These differences in the use of critical are also found in social work; however, in this text critical social work generally refers to a range of perspectives including anti-racist, feminist, social model of disability, anti-oppressive, radical and structural approaches to practice. According to Healy (2000) and others, critical theory emerged from theorists from the Frankfurt Institute, and has been used to shape forms of social work theory and practice. Ife (2005: 55) identifies some important characteristics of critical social work in this way: 'First, critical social work is, by its very nature, critical of at least some aspects of the society within which it is practiced. It refuses to accept the status quo, but rather seeks to effect some kind of social, economic, political or cultural change.' The author goes on to make connections between social change, social movements and the attributes of a 'critical social worker.' This critical social work model seeks to understand the personal in terms of the political and the other way around.

McDonald (2006) argues that early critical social work was influenced by Marxist theory, leading to Bailey and Brake's popular text, *Radical Social Work* (1975), published in the 1970s. During this timeline, radical social work took on a socio-political stance to counter individualized approaches to social problems which tended to offer judgments and blame about moral failings. Yet, whatever its origins, according to Fook (1993), radical traditions shaping critical social work share the same common themes of:

- Examining personal problems through the lens of structural analysis.
- Critically looking at the social control functions of social work and welfare.
- Ongoing social critique of oppressive structures and functions in society.
- Practice tied to social change and personal liberation.

Radical social work perceived the possibilities of social work as a positive agent of social change. Here socialist ideas were harnessed to bring about a more equal society, some of which remain today through the growth of empowerment and consciousness raising practice theories.

Of course, social work is practiced in vastly different welfare contexts around the world, but in recent years, models of welfare in Western countries have gradually moved towards embracing the idea of free markets as the best way to achieve human well-being. From its early beginnings, the profession has struggled with its mission and purpose of individual, group and community well-being at the core of its activities. It is almost taken for granted that social justice work is a major component of social work, yet the current climate in which social work takes place emphasizes personal responsibility for life's eventualities. Even though social work activities continue to be challenged in these ways, questions about equality and greater justice issues remain, demanding new and changing approaches to practice. Some authors have argued that current reforms to social work practice have reduced the possibilities for critical practice, while others view these changes as opportunities to explore the potential of evolving developments in practice (McDonald and Jones, 2000; Healy, 2000).

In the past, the threads of critical theory often aligned with social movements have filtered into social work, fitting neatly into the politics of social change. Pozzuto (2000) reviews these contributions in a useful way by showing that critical work is more than just being 'critical' of the status quo because with a social justice remit, this perspective imagines possible alternative futures through working for progressive social change. Several theorists such as Marx have helped to direct our attention to economic structures and material conditions of life; other theorists direct our gaze to ideology and stratification within cultural life. Foucault has focused attention on the strong connections between knowledge and power. Critical approaches in social work have emerged from these beginnings with multiple strands across different areas which capture a diversity of social justice issues and oppressions. Since postmodern approaches have stripped away collective under-standings of identity and simple ideas of power as fixed and possessed, core themes

in anti-racist, feminist, anti-oppressive, structural multicultural and disability orientations have been called into question. Part of the problem is the lumping together
of social categories as homogenous groups. This is particularly problematic even
accounting for a revised postmodern approach to critical race studies (CRS).
Evolving through legal studies, this field strived to build a platform for theorizing
race as a well-established field in line with gender and class. While race and ethnicity
have been instrumental in documenting structural and institutional inequalities
forging through social changes as an emancipatory project that is ongoing, there is
a lingering association with past definitions of racism associated almost exclusively
with skin color. This association is thorny because the past language of 'race' is
rooted in different national, socio-political and economic contexts, often without
any common agreement about its use, yet as Williams and Graham (2013) note,
these meanings and attributions we give to diverse groups have considerable implications not only for access to rights and inclusion but also to monitoring equality.
In addition, as Noble (2005) suggests, struggles over representation have emerged
as internal differences of gender and class unsettle 'black as a racial category,'
directing focus to the body to display and promote black identities. CRS carries a
postmodern development moving beyond simplistic binary categories and essentialism
to embrace models of intersectionality. This shift reflects the changing nature of
ethnic identities as societies are increasingly multilingual, multifaith and multiethnic,
together with the growth of mixed ethnicities, intermarriage, hybridity and intersections of culture. This dynamic has challenged previous simplistic formulations
and ideas of homogenous ethnic and racial communities toward a more fluid,
nuanced and changing reconfiguration of communities, one which calls for new
terminologies, frames of reference and adaptation to new realities (Williams and
Graham, 2013). In all of this, it is worth remembering that ideas about majority
cultures are also under closer scrutiny, as they can no longer be hidden or perceived
as neutral or homogenous. A subdivision within CRS has emerged, researching
with a focus on how white identities as social constructs operate within racial
hierarchies and often pass unnoticed within dimensions of privilege and power (see
for example, Christie, 2010; and Jeyasingham, 2012).

Given the interlocking nature of oppression, its complexity and shifting relations
of power, a more nuanced understanding of the multiplicity of oppressions and the
way in which they vary in frequency, intensity and pervasiveness is more useful.
This new approach to CRS has developed into an umbrella framework for Latino
critical studies, critical race feminism, critical queer studies and critical white studies
to name a few. As an emerging approach in crafting social work practice, references
to CRS are limited in social work generally (see work of Razack and Jeffery, 2002;
Ortiz and Jani, 2010; Campbell, 2014). Masocha (2015) points to one of the
drawbacks of CRS with its incomplete connections for Indigenous and diaspora
communities with experiences of colonialism linked to oppression and domination.
Gray et al. (2013) lay out a framework for indigenous social work, drawing on
postcolonial theory to revisit, remember and interrogate colonial past. Said's (1979)
widely acclaimed work on colonialism and imperialism held that colonialism does

not end, as its aftermath continues on through postcolonial amnesia suppressing versions of knowledge and agency. Having a critical lens for critical approaches can unravel their shortcomings to extend and modify areas of omission or outdated understandings.

Another point in this discussion is ongoing concern about challenges for practitioners in attempting to translate these perspectives into practice. Although the gap between theory and practice generally continues to be difficult to bridge in social work, structural approaches associated with inequalities and oppression have been particularly tricky. For example, couched as a new practice model, anti-oppressive practice (AOP) held promise as an approach that chimed with social work ambitions of social justice and equality (Dominelli, 2002). This practice model, with its person-centered perspective bringing together individual assistance and working to challenge issues on a structural level, has been subject to intense criticism (see Baines, 2002). AOP has also been subject to criticism from within the profession, revealing how it is easy to examine power, oppression and inequality on a structural level but quite a different matter to translate these lofty goals on the practice front in diverse settings (Williams and Graham, 2016). Beresford and Wilson (2000) examined AOP from a service user (client) perspective, arguing that this approach has failed to engage critically with social work's own position and practices and to ask who determines what is defined as anti-oppressive practice in the first place. Aspirations embedded in social work do not necessarily resonate with everyday practice and the experiences and narratives of people receiving services to frame practice activities. For Beresford (2012), the service user becomes lost in the pursuit of theory and it is possible that anti-oppressive practice can reproduce the very oppression it claims to diminish by being tied to ideology and scholarship rather than knowledge from the ground up (Sakamoto and Pitner, 2005). What is important is to take clients' experiences and narratives to frame practice activities. It is within this context that there has been a declining interest in structural forms of discrimination across social arenas.

More on critical race studies through a postmodern lens

Feminist and anti-racist approaches to social work have taken on these critical postmodern themes with an eye on the differences within these social categories as well as the intersections in social context and situation. For example, CRS under the umbrella of anti-racist approaches to social work is located beyond the black/ white paradigm and essentialism to theorize through intersectionality which speaks to the unique experiences of multiple and intersecting identities of a person. Building upon the growing acceptance of 'studies' in academic institutions, CRS has latched onto this model to reset thinking, taking in social construction, cultural dimensions and meaning in social life where situated identities connected with race, class and gender are created and performed (Denzin, 1999). This field reaches out across boundaries to create a more comprehensive perspective, integrating knowledge from a range of disciplines. Because CRS is working toward adopting a more postmodern lens, extending and revising established models attending to social agency, subjective experiences and meaning in the context of everyday life. Building upon the growing acceptance of 'studies' as interdisciplinary fields in academic institutions, these lines of enquiry include narratives, text, subjective experiences, representations, cross-cultural perspectives and multiple interpretations of lived experiences which recognize that 'people are active, competent interpreters and theorisers of their own lives and those of other people ... and also recognizes that the marginal and disenfranchised are as capable of representing self as those who are more powerful' (Stanley, 2013: 5–6). It is reasonable to argue that the 'everyday' is frequently absent in academic theorizing even though this approach can reveal the complexities of everyday experiences. Some researchers have explored this field in relation to gender inequality coined as 'everyday sexism' to reveal the complexities of everyday experiences. On social media, sharing experiences of 'everyday' sexism and racism on various websites has received a lot of attention in recent times (Powell and Sang, 2015). These approaches seek to uncover the enduring nature of taken-for-granted subtle social relations and practices which can render racism and sexism as invisible and undercover. In this dynamic, Layla speaks about CRS in her narrative as providing a frame of understanding to interrogate her life experiences in the space between intersections of gender and race. Layla describes her reluctance early on to engage in reflection as this could be a trigger for 'uncomfortable feelings' of being positioned as the 'other' in various contexts and settings. Yet as Johns (2009) suggests, reflection is not an end in itself but a journey to realize a vision as a lived reality grounded in holism. Layla's story draws upon counter-narratives as a way of empowering self as well as theories of social construction in understanding and bridging personal and broader social and political arrangements. In examining her own voice she points to the lack of attention given to development and sustaining self in the professional world.

In the face of the declining interest in anti-racist and ethnic minority perspectives in social work, CRS provides strong connections with past critical voices in feminist and anti-racist approaches often linked to wider political struggles, building alliances for social justice issues. One of the points of critique given to the CRS project is the language of race and its tendency to shore up simple black/white social categories and a privileging of racialized minorities over others who occupy the margins of society (for ongoing debates see Bhatti-Sinclair, 2011). CRS as an evolving field (and of course most fields using a 'studies' field are in the same place) attempts to push postmodern approaches to understanding systems of power in social arrangements linked to personal and professional narratives of everyday lived experiences.

Fook's postmodern model of critical social work and reflective practice

Postmodern perspectives are quietly undermining social work theories in helping to shift examination of social structures and depoliticizing social action to studies of social meaning and individual identities (Noble, 2004). In discussing the limitations of structural theories and how they might be implemented on the practice floor, Fook (2002: 7) presents a narrative of her own account of the ways in which structural approaches have been practiced and experienced. She says: 'it was clear to me that whilst radical approaches to social work big-heartedly acknowledged the need for individual work, and personal care, the development of detailed models and strategies for practice remained token.' Here Fook (2002) identifies the limits of these perspectives for guiding radical and critical practice in current human services agencies. This concern is shared by others as a constant challenge to practice in the face of growing inequality in society. Fook (2005: 232) asks the question: 'how can critical social work be defined to allow room for the working out of these tensions?'

With recognition of the complex and contextual character of current social work practice, Fook, amongst others, draws on postmodern perspectives to 'create new possibilities for dialogue between those who practice social work and those who build formal knowledge about it' (Healy, 2005: 221). As Fook seeks to straddle the mismatch between the bigger picture of structural approaches, not just for critical thinking but also the infusion of critical theory in reflective practice to push through the profession's ambitions of social justice on the practice floor. Fook's approach strives to bridge the gap between personal experiences in practice and broader social and political contexts based on the assumption that domination is created structurally but experienced personally. This perspective pays attention to 'the ability to understand the social dimensions and political functions of experience and meaning making, and the ability to apply this understanding to working in social contexts' (Fook, 2010: 45).

Of course, as mentioned earlier in this chapter, the critical in critical reflection terms is associated with many meanings and variations of reflection which shape a range of perspectives. Unraveling meanings underpinning theories across professional fields can be mind-boggling yet there is a common approach to heighten the conscious self-awareness of social, political, cultural and economic contexts of practice. Fook (2010) offers a nuanced understanding of the 'critical,' bringing an integrated understanding to the individual in social realms including workplaces, professional cultures, social, cultural and political contexts. This approach to critical reflection moves beyond individualized versions of reflective practice to contemporary understanding of power as multi-dimensional and key to social work practice questioning how power plays out in our own experiences and individual thinking. By linking these elements through learning from experience, critical abilities can be transferred to everyday practice.

Fook (2002) seeks to drive an integrated approach, one which does not play up to either collective or individual contexts but instead proposes an understanding of critical reflective practice as an intersection and process that starts with the individual. Understanding and working with professional cultures also plays a part in professional learning, particularly in the current climate where there are expectations of grounding practice in particular localized contexts. Fook alerts us to workplace cultures, where there are organizational values in which individuals and organizations construct each other. Looking at the literature on critical reflection, it is clear that there are many strands working in concert, which include:

> how people engage with their worlds and construct a sense of self; how people make meaning from experience in order to guide action; how social structures and relations (including gendered ones) mediate and create personal experiences; and, more specifically, how professionals construct their knowledge and identities within a workplace context.
>
> *(Fook, 2010: 41)*

According to Fook the individual is a microcosm of the social with an awareness of the operation of the social in personal experience. In this context, 'change is thus effected in the individual's social world through a change of individual orientation towards social ideologies/discourses and their effects on the individual' (Fook, 2010: 41). In this process of critical reflection Fook (2010) takes several theoretical approaches including reflective practice, postmodern understandings of power, narrative and language, as well as critical social science to contribute to a broad-base framework. The framework has three guiding themes:

- The individual in their social context.
- Linking theory and practice in critical reflection.
- Linking awareness and action for social change.

In offering a more nuanced approach, Fook (2002) suggests this broader framework for reflective thinking and practice which involves resistance, deconstruction, challenge and social change. The starting point for this process involves questioning to identify and challenge dominant discourses and to see how they are implicated in supporting each other to open up alternative perspectives, co-productions.

Emotional work and reflective practice

Social work is a relationship-based profession and as such, emotions play an important role in interactions and experiences on the practice front. Indeed, the daily life of social workers is 'suffused with emotional content' (Howe, 2008: 13). Emotions are always at play and operating through personal levels of engagement and therefore can have a significant impact upon our decisions, actions and experience of practice (Ingram, 2015). The emotional aspect of practice is filled with contention rooted in the uneasy alliance between rational thought and our emotions wrapped up with professionalism to maintain distance from feelings when faced with emotionally charged situations. The subject of emotions has only recently come to the attention of researchers as emotions are often ignored, suppressed or glossed over, perhaps because they may interfere with tasks in hand (Clarke et al., 2015). Social workers are expected to cope with their emotions and manage them in various ways as part of their professional outlook and competence. Introducing the term emotional labor, Hochschild (2003) defines this work as the amount of effort involved when engaging in face-to-face contact with the public by professions such as social workers. Studsrod (2013: 2) explains: 'the worker who does emotional labour is required to produce an emotional state in another person, such as for instance … feelings of security, hope or pride. Emotional labour has to do with dealing with one's emotions, and could be described as "feeling management" performed as paid work.'

Several authors have raised questions about the lack of attention to the general topic of emotions, not only in social work practice but also in education contexts where this issue is folded into reflective practice (Ikebuchi and Rasmussen, 2014). Trends in sociology have opened up the field of emotions to examine the ways in which emotions are regulated in cultural and social structures through 'rules of feelings' in organizational contexts where relational work requires professionals such as social workers to manage their own emotions according to the societal roles mapped out in professional contexts. Social workers often suppress emotions deemed to be inappropriate and instead present a surface 'face' in line with 'rules of feelings' learned through professional training and education. These disconnections arise when social representations of social workers depict them as being supportive, empathic and warm in the face of emotionally challenging and difficult situations. After all, a social worker's basic duty is to provide emotional support to clients. Social workers experience the greatest stress when they have to suppress their own emotions and act in ways that are contrary to their values and beliefs (Studsrod, 2013).

In recent years, the concept of emotional intelligence has been drawn into service as a proactive strategy of awareness about the use of emotions in social work relationships. Here, these approaches are applied to assist practitioners to understand how emotions affect them as they engage with people often in distressing circumstances with pressing needs. Ingram (2015: 898) refers to emotional intelligence as 'the ability to identify and manage the emotional responses within oneself and in others.' He links emotional intelligence with opportunities for critical reflection as well as the importance of supervision to allow practitioners to consider emotional aspects of practice.

A consistent theme in this chapter has been the links between reflection, reflective practice, personal stories and knowledge of self. It is worthwhile reiterating here the intimate connections between emotions and interpersonal aspects of practice. Reflection engages with emotional awareness and responses to practice. Emotion as the anchor to self-understanding and a central human experience is a thread for continuing self-exploration. Johns and Freshwater (2005: 101) advocate the importance of exploring the intersection of disconnections implicated in the 'rules of feelings' to try to understand emotional reactions and identify those reactions for future practice as a specialized form of knowledge. They go on to articulate their own difficulties with rules of practice (in nursing) which insist on no involvement with patients, and understanding the internal compass of feelings and emotions enables practitioners 'to navigate their way through the daily challenges of clinical practice.' They suggest the understanding of its movement and its rhythm between engagement and disengagement with feelings (using the terms attachment and detachment) are an important learning aspect of reflective activity. In this context, reflective activity can help to strengthen capacity to dissolve emotional load in undertaking care work.

Much has been written about increasing emphasis on paperwork and procedures in contemporary social work, leaving behind aspects of relationship-based inter-ventions and 'emotional reactions of the "heart" ... as emotions can slip down the bureaucratic agenda ... distorting, manipulating, redirecting and neutralizing emo-tion' (Collins, 2007, 258). At this point, it goes without saying that positive and meaningful emotions are also part and parcel of social work practice, and as Collins (2007) notes, positive emotions are common in difficult situations and an integral part of coping and maintaining 'emotional resilience' described as 'the general capacity for flexibility and resourceful adaptation to external and internal stressors' (Klohen, 1996: 1067, quoted in Collins, 2007: 256). Whilst attention has been paid to emotional labor and the ways in which everyday professional life can induce stressful situations, understanding of positive emotions and resilience can prepare students to cope more readily with the demands of the job. As Collins (2007) notes, there is more than one approach to support social workers in dealing with stress in their professional lives.

Conclusion

This chapter began by tracing the development of reflective practice and making connections with back stories shaping its framework and activities. Even though reflective practice has a longstanding place in social work education and practice, there are still some murmurings of unease about the concept, particularly related to the areas of assessment and evaluation. Models of reflection have taken a post-modern lens, posing questions about the social work project itself, resulting in greater scrutiny of practice and professional life. Thinking about one's social posi-tion and where experiences place them in social divisions is all part of developing skills in reflection. Despite the wide range of topics covered in this chapter, the themes of self-awareness, reflection and critical theory are discussed with connec-tions to agency and voice to highlight the importance of context and everyday experiences set in narrative projects.

References

Argyris, C. and Schön, D. (1974) *Theory in practice: increasing professional effectiveness*, San Francisco: Jossey-Bass.

Bager-Charleson, S. (2010) *Reflective practice in counselling and psychotherapy*, London: Sage.

Bailey, R. and Brake, M. (1975) *Radical social work*, London: Edward Arnold.

Baines, D. (2002) 'Race, class and gender in the everyday talk of social workers: the ways we limit the possibilities for radical practice,' *Race Gender and Class Journal*, 9(1): 145–167.

Beres, L. (2014) *The narrative practitioner*, London: Palgrave Macmillan.

Beresford, P. (2012) 'Service-user involvement.' In M. Gray, J. Midgley and S. Webb (eds), *The Sage handbook of social work*, London: Sage, pp. 693–706.

Beresford, P. and Wilson, A. (2000) 'Anti-oppressive practice, emancipation or appropriation,' *British Journal of Social Work*, 30(5): 553–573.

Bhatti-Sinclair, K. (2011) *Anti-racist practice in social work*, Basingstoke: Palgrave Macmillan.

Biestek, F.P. (1961) *The casework relationship*, London: Allen and Unwin.

Bolton, G. (2005) *Reflective practice, writing and professional development*, London: Sage.

Bradbury, H., Frost, N., Kilminster, S. and Zukas, M. (2010) *Beyond reflective practice: new approaches to professional lifelong learning*, London: Routledge.

Brown, C. and Augusta-Scott, T. (2007) *Narrative therapy, making meaning, making lives*, Thousand Oaks: Sage Publications.

Campbell, E. (2014) 'Using critical race theory to measure "racial" competence among social workers,' *Journal of Sociology and Social Welfare*, 2(2): 73–86.

Christie, A. (2010) 'Whiteness and the politics of "race" in child protection guidelines in Ireland,' *European Journal of Social Work*, 13(2): 199–217.

Clarke, C., Broussine, M. and Watts, L. (2015) *Researching with feeling: the emotional aspects of social and organizational research*, London: Routledge.

Collins, S. (2007) 'Social workers, resilience, positive emotions and optimism,' *Practice: Social Work in Action*, 19(4): 255–269.

Combs, G. and Freedman, J. (2012) 'Narrative, poststructuralism and social justice: current practices in narrative therapy,' *The Counseling Psychologist*, 40(7): 1033–1060.

Cooper, B. and Broadfoot, P. (2006) 'Beyond description and prescription towards a conducive assessment in social work education,' *International Studies in Sociology of Education*, 16(2): 139–157.

Damron-Rodriguez, J. (2008) 'Developing competence for nurses and social workers,' *Journal of Social Work Education*, 44(3): 27–37.

Danto, E. (2008) 'Some words, different meanings: notes toward a typology of postmodern social work education,' *Social Work Education*, 27(7): 710–722.

Denzin, N. (1999) 'From American sociology to cultural studies,' *European Journal of Cultural Studies*, 1(2): 117–136.

Dominelli, L. (2002) *Anti-oppressive social work theory and practice*, New York: Palgrave Macmillan.

Dominelli, L. (2007) 'The postmodern "turn" in social work: the challenges of identity and equality,' *Social Work and Society, International Online Journal*, 5(3).

Epston, D. and White, M. (1992) *Experience, contradiction, narrative and imagination: selected papers of David Epston and Michael White, 1989–1991*. Adelaide, South Australia: Dulwich Centre Publications.

Fook, J. (1993) *Radical casework: A theory of practice*, St Leonards, Australia: Allen and Unwin.

Fook, J. (2002) *Social work: a critical theory and practice*, London: Sage.

Fook, J. (2005) 'Challenges and directions for critical social work.' In S. Hick, J. Fook and R. Puzzuto (eds), *Social work: a critical turn*, Toronto: Thompson Educational, pp. 231–237.

Fook, J. (2010) 'Beyond reflective practice: reworking the "critical" in critical reflection.' In H. Bradbury, N. Frost, S. Kilminster and M. Zukas (eds), *Beyond reflective practice: new approaches to professional lifelong learning*, London: Routledge, pp. 37–51.

Fook, J. (2012) 'The challenges of creating critically reflective groups,' *Social Work with Groups*, 35: 218–234.

Foucault, M. (1972) *The archaeology of knowledge and the discourse on language*, New York: Pantheon Books.

Gardner, F. (2014) *Being critically reflective*, Basingstoke: Palgrave Macmillan.

Gould, N. and Taylor, I. (1996) *Reflective learning for social work: research, theory and practice*, Aldershot: Ashgate.

Graham, M. and Schiele, J. (2010) 'Anti-discriminatory and equality of oppressions models in social work: reflections from the UK and USA,' *European Journal of Social Work*, 13(2): 231–244.

Gray, M., Coates, J. and Yellowbird, M. (2013) *Decolonizing social work*, Surrey: Ashgate.

Healy, K. (2000) *Social work practices: contemporary perspectives on change*, London: Sage.

Healy, K. (2005) 'Under reconstruction: renewing critical social work practices.' In S. Hick, J. Fook and R. Puzzuto (eds), *Social work: a critical turn*, Toronto: Thompson, pp. 219–230.

Hochschild, A.R. (2003) *The managed heart: commercialization of human feeling*, Berkeley: University of California Press.

Howe, D. (2008) *The emotionally intelligent social worker*, London: Palgrave Macmillan.

Ife, J. (2005) 'Human rights and critical social work.' In S. Hick, J. Fook and R. Puzzuto (eds), *Social work: a critical turn*, Toronto: Thompson, pp. 55–66.

Ikebuchi, J. and Rasmussen, B.M. (2014) 'The use of emotions in social work education,' *Journal of Teaching in Social Work*, 34: 285–301.

Ingram, R. (2015) 'Exploring emotions within formal and informal forums: messages from social work practitioners,' *British Journal of Social Work*, 45(3): 896–913.

Ingram, R., Fenton, J., Hodson, A. and Jinal-Snape, D. (2014) *Reflective social work practice*, London: Palgrave Macmillan.

Ixer, G. (1999) 'There's no such thing as reflection,' *British Journal of Social Work*, 29: 513–527.

Ixer, G. (2010) 'There's no such thing as reflection ten years on,' *Journal of Teaching and Learning*, 10(1): 75–93.

Jeyasingham, D. (2012) 'White noise: a critical evaluation of social work education's engagement with whiteness studies,' *British Journal of Social Work*, 42(4): 669–686.

Johns, C. (2009) *Becoming a reflective practitioner*, London: Wiley.

Johns, C. (2012) 'How holistic are we? The role of narrative, storytelling and reflection in the development of holistic practice,' *European Journal of Cancer Care*, 21: 561–564.

Johns, C. and Freshwater, D. (eds) (2005) *Transforming nursing through reflective practice*, Oxford: Blackwell.

Klohen, E. (1996) 'Conceptual analysis and measurement of the construct of ego resiliency,' *Journal of Personality and Social Psychology*, 70(5): 1067–1079.

Knott, C. (2007) 'Reflective practice revised.' In C. Knott and T. Scragg (eds), *Reflective practice in social work*, UK: Learning Matters, pp. 3–13.

Lavalette, M. (2011) *Radical social work today*, Bristol: Policy Press.

Masocha, S. (2015) 'Reframing black social work students' experiences of teaching and learning,' *Social Work Education*, 34(6): 636–649.

McDonald, C. (2006) *Challenging social work: the context of practice*, London: Palgrave Macmillan.

McDonald, C. and Jones, A. (2000) 'Reconstructing and re-conceptualizing social work in the emerging milieu,' *Australian Social Work*, 53(3): 3–11.

Merrill, B. and West, L. (2009) *Using biographical methods in social research*, Thousand Oaks: Sage.

Murphy, M., Dempsey, M. and Halton, C. (2010) 'Reflective inquiry in social work education.' In N. Lyons (ed.), *Handbook of reflection and reflective inquiry*, New York: Springer, pp. 173–188.

Noble, C. (2004) 'Postmodern thinking: where is it taking social work?' *Journal of Social Work*, 4(3): 289–304.

Noble, D. (2005) 'Remembering bodies, healing histories: the emotional politics of everyday freedom.' In C. Alexander and C. Knowles (eds), *Making race matter, bodies, space and identity*, Basingstoke: Palgrave, pp. 132–152.

Ortiz, L. and Jani, J. (2010) 'Critical race theory: a transformational model for teaching diversity,' *Journal of Social Work Education*, 46(2): 175–193.

Papouli, E. (2014) 'Field learning in social work education: implications for educators and instructors,' *The Field Educator Journal*, Simmons School of Social Work, 4(2): 1–15.

Parton, N. (2002) 'Postmodern and constructionist approaches to social work.' In R. Adams, L. Dominelli and M. Payne (eds), *Social work, themes, issues and critical debates* (2nd edn), London: Palgrave Macmillan, pp. 237–246.

Payne, M. (2002) 'Social work theories and reflective practice.' In R. Adams, L. Dominelli and M. Payne (eds), *Social work, themes, issues and critical debates* (2nd edn), London: Palgrave Macmillan, pp. 123–138.

Payne, M. (2014) *Modern social work theory* (4th edn), Basingstoke: Palgrave Macmillan.

Powell, A. and Sang, K.J. (2015) 'Everyday experiences of sexism in male dominated professions: a Bourdieusian perspective,' *Sociology*, 49(5): 919–936.

Pozzuto, R. (2000) 'Notes on a possible critical social work,' *Critical Social Work*, 1(2): 1–3.

Razack, N. and Jeffery, D. (2002) 'Critical race discourse and tenets for social work,' *Canadian Social Work Review*, 19(2): 257–271.

Rogowski, S. (2010) *Social work: the rise and fall of a profession?* Bristol: Policy Press.

Said, E. (1979) *Orientalism*, New York: Vintage Books.

Sakamoto, I. and Pitner, R.O. (2005) 'Use of critical consciousness in anti-oppressive social work practice: disentangling power dynamics at personal and structural levels,' *British Journal of Social Work*, 35(4): 435–452.

Schön, D. (1983) *The reflective practitioner: how professionals think in action*, New York: Basic Books.

Schön, D. (1987) *Educating the reflective practitioner*, San Francisco: Jossey-Bass.

Stanley, L. (2013) *Documents of life revisited: narrative and biographical methodology for a 21st century critical humanism*, Surrey: Ashgate.

Studsrod, I. (2013) 'Emotional labour and solving social work problems,' Editorial, *Journal of Comparative Social Work*, 8(1): 1–5.

Sztompkai, P. (2008) 'The focus on everyday life: a new turn in sociology,' *European Review*, 16(1): 1–15.

Tangenberg, K. and Kemp, S. (2002) 'Embodied practice, claiming the body's experience, agency and knowledge for social work,' *Social Work*, 47(1): 9–18.

Thompson, S. and Thompson, N. (2008) *The critically reflective practitioner*, Basingstoke: Palgrave Macmillan.

Urdang, E. (2010) 'Awareness of self – a critical tool,' *Social Work Education*, 29, 523–538.

Walker, S. (2001) 'Tracing the contours of postmodern social work,' *British Journal of Social Work*, 31(1): 29–39.

Walmsley, C. and Birbeck, J. (2006) 'Personal narrative writing: a method of values reflection for BSW students,' *Journal of Teaching in Social Work*, 26(1/2).

Williams, C. and Graham, M. (2013) *Social work in Europe*, London: Routledge.

Williams, C. and Graham, M. (2016) *Social work in a diverse society*, Bristol: Policy Press.

3

RESEARCH, NARRATIVE, REFLECTION AND SELF-INQUIRY

Introduction

Social workers as well as other professionals in practice-based disciplines are encouraged to make critical use of research studies, by becoming research practitioners using findings to inform their practice. While each discipline has its own approaches to research, both qualitative and quantitative methods contribute to answering a range of research questions providing a framework for professional practice.

Much has been written about the uneasy and ambivalent relationship between social work and research resulting in long-running debates about the nature and function of social work research across the field. Such tensions have surfaced across multiple levels rooted in a social work knowledge base where the inter-relationships of knowledge creation (research), knowledge transmission (teaching) and knowledge application (practice) inform each other in complex and dynamic ways (Lyons, 2010). It is worthwhile here to look more closely at the definitions of qualitative and quantitative research. Basically, quantitative research is used to describe empirical or positivist research, which generally uses experimentation, statistical data and observation methods to collect data. Qualitative research, on the other hand, relies on non-mathematical data and instead employs interpretive and critical models. In so much of the debate about research, these divisions are often represented as opposite positions in a simple way, yet qualitative researchers can and do utilize quantitative techniques to analyze data. What is evident from a brief review of qualitative research is not only its differing orientations, but also a wide range of different methodologies. The authors Higgs and Cant (1998: 1–2) identify applied forms of qualitative research such as:

- Multiple realities are socially constructed, meaning different people have different perceptions of reality through their ascribed meaning to events, meaning being part of the event, not separate from it.

- The process of inquiry changes both the investigator and the subject/participant.
- Knowledge is both context and time dependent. Quantitative research seeks to uncover generalizations and universal truths, while qualitative research looks for deeper understanding of the particular.
- Qualitative research can describe and interpret events.
- Research inquiry by its very nature is value laden, that is how questions are asked and how results are interpreted, as well as being dependent upon our underlying assumptions about the nature of research.

As an evolving field, qualitative research has moved through several sequences. Denzin and Lincoln (2011) articulate these changes as 'five moments' when qualitative research moved through several phases influenced by feminism, postmodernism, politics, social movements, liberating philosophies, cultural studies, social justice topics and post-colonialism. As a result, qualitative inquiry morphed into a broad developing area across a range of disciplines influencing each other with different forms of interpretative perspectives. These perspectives carry with them particular philosophical foundations that impact the way researchers frame their work.

Ways of knowing

Experiential knowledge is an established outlook bringing recognition to describing experiences in what we take to be reality and often expressed in the form of narratives. 'Lived experience' is a popular term often used to draw attention to how we interpret what happens in our lives as we make sense of our feelings, perceptions and actions. Of further relevance here are particular social conditions integral to specific stages in our lives. By virtue of this context, research as experience is always to be approached with careful examination taking account of the variations of experience, its changeable characteristics moving between who we are and what we know. Pickering (2008: 20) takes up this point, describing different kinds of experience including:

> experiences we choose to have, for whatever reason, and experiences that are imposed on us, sometimes against our will or because they are or seem unavoidable. There are also experiences on which we have reflected deeply and which we have absorbed into our self-knowledge, and others we hardly think about at all … as we go about our everyday lives. Our lives are a peculiar compound of various forms of experience.

In this dynamic we use these forms of experience to develop knowledge about our own lives and the lives of other people. These narrations of experience are by no means straightforward; they are complex, full of contradictions and often 'messy.' In response to marginalized or oppressed groups, their voices and experiences often neglected in research, subjective experience and voice continues to play a pivotal role in opening up space to articulate insights into personal accounts gained through direct experience in everyday life. This line of research takes narrative as its starting point to examine lived experiences through stratification and other oppressive practices in wider society. For example, over many decades, feminist methodology has emphasized the importance of bringing women's voices and personal experiences into the research process. This development recognizes that our personal lives are intertwined in social, political and historical contexts (Ryan, 2001). Ways of knowing drawn from feminist perspectives have pushed through new ways of understanding the human condition by opening up new pathways of knowledge which have hitherto been neglected. Useful insights into women's narratives and personal accounts have helped to untangle the socialized position of gender to examine the ways in which dominant patriarchal ideologies are created, reproduced and resisted in retelling of stories. Postmodern developments have influenced the interpretation of narratives in research, allowing multiple identities and messy narrative 'texts' often resulting in fragmented and conflicting narrative (Falconer, 2009).

One example of knowledge building informed by experiential knowledge is the concept of care in professional practice and its transformation from private concerns into public discussions. These developments have generated a body of literature about the nature of care and caring in society, and particularly its ethical dimensions and understandings. As broader perspectives of care are located within the context of social justice and well-being, social researchers are particularly interested in unraveling its significant features in contemporary social life. In this context, definitions of care are applicable to broader problems of social organization and practice. Tronto (1993: 103) explains:

> On the most general level, we suggest that caring be viewed as a species activity that includes everything that we do to maintain, continue or repair our world so that we can live in it as well as possible. That world includes our bodies, ourselves, and our environment, all of which we seek to interweave in a complex, life sustaining web.

Care is a common word deeply embedded in our everyday language and seems to carry with it two intrinsic features. First, care implies a reaching out to something other than the self; and second, care implicitly suggests that it will lead to some kind of action as an ongoing process. Care has been identified as having four interconnected phases – caring about, taking care of, care giving and receiving care (Tronto, 1993). These understandings of care are understood by Tronto (1993) through a model, which addresses the ethical elements of care. Attentiveness is an ethical element of care and the awareness of the needs of others, and to be attentive to one's own needs, is to understand that all human beings experience this need for care and it is not restricted to 'needy persons.'

Next, the ethical element of responsibility in that attentiveness cannot take place without taking responsibility for action and it is implicit in cultural practices. This approach suggests a broader responsibility for the social and natural environment and our place in it (Fine, 2007). Competence is concerned with the impact of care and as care becomes embedded in bureaucracies sometimes care appears to be performed without any concern for the outcomes (Barnes, 2006). Responsiveness holds that carers must be conscious of the possibilities of abuse that arise with vulnerability and requires attentiveness and the integration of all four elements 'in order to develop knowledge and act in a thoughtful way in relation to the situations, needs and competences of other actors' (Barnes, 2006: 120). This broader understanding of care shifted attention to the elements of care which are identified as a process that can function as a social value and an orientation that defines our being in the world (Tronto, 1993; Graham, 2007). In taking these understandings of care into social and political landscapes, feminists are seeking to disentangle a web of social arrangements and practices to understand moral difference as a function of both social positioning and gender. These background discussions are highly relevant to women of color, where socio-cultural and historical contexts often intersect their everyday lives in different ways.

Of course, there are many differing interests and diversity among women of color, yet lived experiences, as women themselves conceive, is often the starting point for ethical concerns in reclaiming the everyday world. These culturally based ways of knowing are often expressed through strategies of social agency, freedom which deploy and facilitate inner knowing, spiritual knowledge, choosing education for living with deeper awareness of self, consciousness raising and empowerment (Gordon, 2007). Attending to cultural products, themes, symbolic language, self-adornment and other ways of being shapes reclaiming care. There is a close historical and contemporary relationship between women of color and caring activities in the labor market. There is a wealth of research about the life experiences of women of color as workers in the heavy end of care work, both in private households and in the public sphere (Coble, 2006; Hunter, 1998). Several authors have also examined the representations of women of color created in the wider society, which include the all giving and 'natural' carers/servants supporting their social subordination (Hill-Collins, 2000; Beauboeuf-Lafontant, 2007).

However, women of color sometimes draw upon cultural self-care and knowledge to create conditions for empowering self-definitions in which consciousness can become a sphere of freedom. Noble (2005) suggests that 'new' liberation struggles are emerging from individualized acts of resistance through the re-creation of black identities that are concerned with social relationships, states of mind, health and body. Many of these discourses are apparent in the popularity of self-development programs, books and workshops which advocate self-knowledge, embedding process in life, nurturing the internal world (spirit), holism and seeking support through collaboration with others (Gordon, 2001). Self-determination and freedom have long been sites of resistance and empowerment in everyday action and experience. In this context, Noble (2005: 135) explores the 'everyday tactics that some black women deploy to empower themselves in struggles against the various individuals, groups, institutions and systems that they understand as blocking their path to autonomy, self-determination of freedom.'

Reading the student narratives of Layla, Nicole and Vanessa in the second part of the book brings some of these points to bear in rising to sensory understandings in their everyday lives allowing for meanings and experiences to emerge through cultural self-care and affirmation. These tools create conditions of empowerment embedded in counter-narratives. Noble (2005) suggests that these empowerment strategies are responding to multiple caring responsibilities which many women of color undertake and as a mark of resistance to negative stereotypes that seek to blame them for the ills within their communities. In this way, caring labor is transformed into a source of power rather than victimization and devaluation. These developments frame the backdrop of research and wider understandings of care and care giving. As care is strongly linked to social welfare, including com-munity-based support, there are social and political implications about the nature of society and how it is organized.

I have mentioned earlier that research is inextricably tied up with understanding about conceptions of knowledge, which brings within it complex processes of interpretations and styles. So even choosing a research approach raises several issues. Higgs and Cant (1998) believe that although researchers should be channeling professionals with useful knowledge for practice, this is sometimes not the case. They argue that it is well recognized that the type of knowledge gleaned from research is dependent upon the model of research adopted by researchers, and the creation of knowledge is dynamic, related to particular circumstances, times and social constructs. Finally, in an earlier section, I have stated that there are multiple knowledge sources and ways of knowing drawing on increasingly interdisciplinary contexts and overlapping fields. Before I go further, that social work's knowledge base also stems from a variety of sources in the social and human sciences including sociology, psychology and psychiatry, amongst others, is acknowledged with all their various research approaches cutting across disciplines.

Historical influences, social work, knowledge and research

Notwithstanding these series of starting points, the early development of the profession has had considerable influence on approaches to research in social work. This scenario played out as alliances were forged with scientific models of knowledge building to gain and enhance social recognition and status as an emerging profession. During the nineteenth century, the central mission of the social work project involved throwing off the shackles of moralizing, charity, philanthropic and religious objectives to embrace a more secular outlook, tied to a rational account of the human condition and social improvement. Here, the profession was caught up in a period when scien-tific models of research approaches held sway with promise that their application would provide solutions to social problems. In this context, a new class of profes-sionals developed, with expertise gained through education and 'rooted in a body of knowledge which could be acknowledged as scientific' (Bowpitt, 1998: 693).

Lorenz (2011) argues that the contentious issues related to qualitative and quantitative research methods continue to be linked with social work's professional identity and perhaps more so in the current climate when trends point to a fragmentation of the profession and the discipline. Past debates have grappled with questions about social work as an occupation, in two distinct ways, as an art or as a science, mainly drawing on the qualitative methods for the former and quantitative methods for the latter set of dynamics. There are, of course, intersections of building and retaining professional status juxtaposed with 'retaining the empowering elements of voluntarism and solidarity with users' (Lorenz, 2011: 49). Reconciling these tensions between research approaches that have creative and interpretative potential and those based on scientific rigor continue to drive debates within the profession where resolution is not easily realized. Social and political realities also come into play here, as evidence-based practice with the promise of measurements, reliability and transparency of actions has filtered into the landscape linked to more public accountability of the profession. Some of the critiques surrounding evidence-based practice support the lack of wider social, political and economic contexts, producing a partial view in research-based practice.

On top of these dynamics, as qualitative research dominates the social work research scene, this form of knowledge has a tendency to be viewed in academic and institutional entities as weak, 'soft data' alongside the 'scientific rigor' uptake of evidence-based informed practice. In the wake of many discussions on this point, McDonald (2006: 159) comments that 'one of the major justifications for the promotion of evidence based practice is the desire of its proponents to lift social work out of what is presented as a quagmire of irrationality.' Others claim the rise of evidence-based practice is in response to government agendas that claim practice should be informed by research evaluations on effectiveness and accountability (see McDonald, 2006 for a review of this discussion). Suffice to say, in resolving this dilemma mixed methods are often used, bringing evidence-based and qualitative approaches together in a single research study as a step in the right direction to resolving this debate. On a broader front, these issues are situated in controversies about how knowledge should be defined, generating questions such as what is knowledge? How do we know? What do we choose to know and what ways of knowing do we explore? Other issues of relevance here are who decides what counts as research and the value attached to specific kinds of research in the hierarchy of knowledge structures; furthermore, what models should be applied to generate new knowledge? This muddy landscape forms the backdrop to social work research where postmodern ideas have re-emphasized the relationship between power and knowledge pushing forms of research into service that are contextual inside local practice from the ground up linked to the emancipatory potential of research activities.

Research practice – opening up areas of experience

Recently, new areas of qualitative research have emerged, found in cultural studies and its experiential models of analysis, bringing a deeper context to ethnographic projects. These experimental research designs are orientated towards social creativity using methodologies such as fiction, poetry, drama, performance and novellas where research participants are collaborators (Bryant, 2015). Bryant (2015: 2) suggests this revision of how we think about research has been brought about by the complexities of modern life and the need to pause to take a reflexive outlook and space to question 'our place as one who asks questions and attempts to answer them.' Research orientated in creative inquiry takes working with communities of people as its anchor to improve social conditions and transform lives. It goes without saying that various participant research methods have long been an important way of working in collaboration with groups and communities with many positive outcomes. Creative inquiry in research moves to fill in the gaps shifting away from scientific models of collection to one of discovery, moving research out of comfort zones to thrive on the 'edge of things' (Bryant, 2015). This edge of things refers to methods that capture imagination, emotion, visual and textual methods, including performance. Capturing emotions and contradictory meanings is expressed in forms of art and poetry, as Bryant (2015: 11) explains, acknowledging 'space for the emotional and sensory to emerge in ways that may not occur or may not be allowed for in traditional interviews.'

These recent trends have also emphasized a reflexive role of the researcher. Such an approach calls on researchers to consider their own relationship to the study and background to connect with political concerns as much as voice and narrative. Here there are many conversations going on about 'the degree to which the researcher should place her/his voice within a sociopolitical context' (Roberts, 2002: 14). Most of the concerns outlined earlier are tied to a critical model of knowledge and research, one in which the importance of insight, reflexivity and meaning is interactions. These developments reflect the higher profile of qualitative research, specifically the attention to the stages in research as a process involving the complex relations in design, collection of data, theoretical frameworks as the researcher moves between these dynamic and complex areas (Roberts, 2002). Within this process, researchers reflect upon their own story to gain insights into experiences and feelings involved in research to bring them to the surface, in this process of meaning making to understand interactions in encounters as they influence and shape each other. The reflexive nature of research is wrapped in social critique concerning the power imbalance between the researcher and participant recognizing multiple shifting of positions (Finlay, 2002).

Of interest here is the writing of research, as a narrative of both the method and experience critically examining methods in subjective contexts. Emerging issues arising during the research process itself come to light crafting experiences, interpretations in different styles as research as it is lived. As Roberts (2002: 48) notes, 'the writing of research can be likened to a literary exercise in expression which can take various forms – descriptive, analytic, fantasy, comic, realistic, romantic, philosophical and so on – of presentation.' The traditional view of the researcher as objective, researching from a distance, is replaced with insightful accounts of a series of experiences using the metaphor of a journey: rather than the destination, it is the journey itself.

Johns (2010) also frames narrative as a journey of self-inquiry with emphasis on being and becoming through reflection on research practice pushing forward the idea that reflective practice is at the center of narrative inquiry. In this re-evaluation of research and researcher relations, emotions and feelings are welcomed along the journey of research practice. In many ways, emotional experiences in research practice have been more or less discounted or at the very least put on the back burner. Clarke et al. (2015) say the prevailing view in academic circles leans towards avoiding researchers' own feelings and experiences because they can interfere with the task at hand and need to be constrained and managed. Despite a growing interest in emotions in research practice, these discussions are limited in mainstream research literature. Clarke et al. (2015) advocate reclaiming and writing this work into research practice, particularly when researchers find their research work often more complex and challenging than articulated in methodology texts.

Higgs and Llewellyn (1998) describe critical and interpretative models as conveying awareness of how our thinking is socially and historically constructed and passing on limitations in our actions. In other ways, this model encourages people to challenge their assumptions and learned restrictions to acquire knowledge through critical debate. This framework 'promotes understanding about how to transform current structures, relationships and conditions which constrain development and reform' (Higgs and Llewellyn, 1998: 61). Brew (1998: 9) lays out clearly our understanding of research as constructed by our subject or discipline in the wider academic community as well as 'what research is and what they are doing when they carry it out.' This participatory strategy begins not only with our understanding of the nature of research itself, models and methods but also the process of framing research questions. In a study undertaken by Higgs and Llewellyn (1998), student participants were interviewed about the process of framing research questions in the context of education:

> Framing the question was quite a challenge. I didn't know what questions to ask. First I had to listen to my participants talking about their experiences. Then I started to develop understanding of … and I was able to derive some questions.
>
> *(Higgs and Llewellyn, 1998: 66)*

> I'm the most comfortable with the critical paradigm because it helps me to look at my own actions as well as those of others – other colleagues, practitioners or patients. (I want) to help them become empowered to act in a way that they would like to and action research enables them to dismantle the constraints and the taken-for-granted constraints which are often there which prevent them doing what they want or acting in the way they would like to act, rather than in the way they have been socialized into.
>
> A key issue for me in doing research is that the methodological framework I adopt needs to be compatible with my own theoretical framework.
>
> *(Higgs and Llewellyn, 1998: 65)*

Research practice and social justice ambitions

Following this line of discussion also brings to mind ethical research practice and the ways in which this commitment is related to the profession's obligations to social justice and human rights. Humphries (2008) argues that principles of human rights and social justice are at the heart of social work practice and it does not make sense that they should not be applied to social work research. Writing in this vein she notes:

> Ethical social work research that is committed to social justice cannot sustain an unquestioning acceptance of received definitions of social problems, or simply measure the outcomes of social experiments without having an eye to the bigger context, and without asking about the origins, motivations and intended uses of such research ... A research commitment not to be impartial to human suffering, to identify unjust (not just inefficient) processes and make them known, to ensure that subordinated voices are heard and heeded, are entirely compatible with the best traditions of rigorous and systematic research approaches.
>
> *(Humphries, 2008: 31)*

I have included this long quotation written because it succinctly encapsulates a view of social justice research. Such debates echo Lorenz's (2011) point about the need for developing a coherent research knowledge base with practice. Through its wide range of methods, it is well suited to exploring questions that relate to meaning of experiences and understanding the complexities of human behavior. This relationship-based approach allows researchers to connect with people, often in deep and meaningful ways, describing their actions, thoughts and events in their lives (Gilgun and Abrams, 2002). For the most part, the proficiency needed in collecting data is easily applied in social work where interviewing and observations are core practice skills learned through education and practice. While qualitative methodology tends to align with social work tasks and activities, this method also produces materials such as clinical tools, case studies as well as rich descriptions of current and past events, which are useful to direct practice. Another worthwhile consideration is its connections with theory, building from the ground up in knowledge production to enable subjective experiences and voice to be given precedence to find meaning behind statistics. These approaches create interpretative and creative potential taking a practice-focused reflexivity. Some of the key characteristics of qualitative research are:

- Understanding people's social world, their personal and lived experiences.
- Researching in context.
- Research undertaken in its natural setting.
- Interactive process.
- Distinct research methods.

- Open to theoretical challenges.
- Longitudinal elements.

Across the decades, there has been a great deal of debate about the merits and challenges of qualitative inquiry. These challenges are still very much with us, continuing to raise many questions about qualitative research including concerns about its wide-ranging loose approaches, 'where it is sometimes hard to see the relationship between what various qualitative scholars do. They use very different kinds of texts ... They also treat texts in radically different ways' (Riessman, 1994: xii, quoted in Shaw and Gould, 2001: 8).

Narrative research

Narrative research is one of these broad developing areas offering scope for new accounts of the individual, including life story, self-inquiry, personal experience, auto-ethnography, autobiography, discourse, ethnography and self-reflection. These interesting explorations are strongly connected to postmodern insights making for different sources about the stuff of life and allowing real experiences to come alive in a unique way. From an extensive social science base, interest in individual experiences of everyday life has contributed to this growing interest in narrative employed in many other disciplinary fields such as history and literature. These trends have been described as a 'narrative moment' in social research (Plummer, 1995b), where personal stories are experienced in changing social and political contexts. While the relevance of personal and professional narratives is evident in popular culture, similar developments have taken place in social movements and activism working towards social and political change.

In asking the question 'what brings people to give voice to this story at this historical movement?' Plummer (1995a: 106) draws more attention to the role of stories and narrative in the wider social and historical contexts over time shifting perceptions of stories simply as a representative of individual life to understanding how the story is produced and consumed. This focus helps us to recognize power relations implicated in storytelling: 'stories are not just practical or symbolic actions; they are also part of the political process ... power is not so much an all or nothing phenomenon, which people either have or don't have, and which resides either here or there. Rather it is best viewed as a flow, a process ... oscillating through the social world and working to pattern the degree of control people experience and have over their lives' (Plummer, 1995b: 26). In framing analysis of stories, Plummer uses social interaction, the development of shared meaning and the political process, in understanding the social role of stories, 'the ways they are produced, the ways they are read, the work they perform in the wider social order, how they change, and their role in the political process.' Plummer (1995b) demonstrates the wider social context in which a story is being told, particularly communities that hear and receive stories because they are implicated in power relations in political processes. Plummer provides a useful model of this wider context of narrative contained in both individual and social life.

Narratives operate from personal, cultural, ethical/moral and political life. In the personal space they bring together and connect with identity shaping, trauma and repair, and therapeutic narratives.

- Cultural: educational, change, issue raising and reproduction of values; dominant narratives and counter-narratives.
- Political: stories of difference, social movements of change, continuum of successful lives to wasted lives.
- Moral/ethical: good and bad life.

Plummer (1995b) notes that listening to the stories of others different from yours is central for democracy to function in societies seeking respect and recognition for human differences. When we hear stories from people who are marginalized or the outsider, 'the other,' these stories deepen our sympathies and understanding of social problems in the world. Stories are often used by activists and reformers as an integral part of social movements to open up possibilities for social change. Narratives bind the personal to the wider society and can enter processes of social change. Although narratives are often perceived as critical and powerful because they bear witness to experiences and can galvanize public support for campaigns around social justice or human rights issues, they also function like any other power and can move in different directions, either for or against inequality.

Taking these wider frames of reference, how are they connected to individual reflective practice and narrative? Lorde, in the popular text *Sister Outsider*, directs this question to personal knowing and reflection in replying: 'the true focus of revolutionary change is never merely the oppressive situations which we seek to escape, but that piece of the oppressor which is planted deep within each of us' (Lorde, 1984: 123). Reflective practice is at the center of narrative and self-inquiry. Furthermore, at the critical edge of reflection is the quest to free ourselves from oppressive forces which often deny the voice of feelings and anxieties that surface in daily living, closing the door to transformation and ways of being free (Johns, 2010). It goes without saying that oppressions are not uniform; they often inhabit simultaneous and contradictory overlapping positions in various social settings. One of the consistent themes of this text has been to explore the ways in which our culture, personal and social histories affect our ways of thinking and shaping our social work selves. Yogita, the narrative in Chapter 7, reflects on her experiences working in the field of practice in a different geographical location with multiple layers of cultural norms and values where learning took place through dialogue. These conversations were not only with her field supervisor but also through reflection, steering and learning about herself in spaces of dialogue. These acts of self-inquiry appreciate and become mindful of self within experience (Johns, 2010).

Freire (1972: 70–73) offers insights into the empowering elements of dialogue because it is 'an encounter among women and men who name the world, it must not be a situation where some name on behalf of others. It is an act of creation … at the point of encounter … there are only people who are attempting, together to learn more than they now know.' In other words, storytelling is a way of participants sharing experiences in their own words and naming their social world. Learning takes place as they develop an understanding of the context where the story takes place, raising collective consciousness. A dialogue that engages in critical thinking 'which discerns an indivisible solidarity between the world and the people which perceives reality as process, as transformation' (Freire, 1972: 73). It is much easier to see oppressive forces 'out there' divorced from the self than acknowledge our own oppression and limitations sometimes found in particular 'habits of mind' (see Margolis, 1993 for definition and discussion of 'habits of mind'). Johns (2010: 11) refers to these modes of thinking as adhering to false beliefs (common-sense ways of looking at the world), infused with meanings that sustain our disempowerment.

The following chapters in the text offer the reader a mix of beginning and evolving personal stories about social work and journeys through social work education from students themselves as they grapple with self-inquiry, unearthing their experiences and sharing their personal stories. It is more about who I am; gaining insight into self as a precursor to finding out how I act in situations as a practitioner. Although these encounters with researching self are dotted with complexity, uncertainty as well as the possibilities of political consciousness, they offer shifts in new action and ways of being in the world shaping a vision of self and practice.

Narrative in research has evolved in tandem with its popular usage, generally leading to qualitative methods providing a useful model for storytelling and personal writing to 'show more about what our understanding really is, how it works and how we construct a system of meanings for our experience' (Cihodariu, 2012: 31). This range of narrative approaches is contested – that is, unlike some other qualitative methods, narrative frames offer little direction in terms of rules about modes of investigation or most suitable level to use for studying stories. Much of this discussion about narrative approaches in research is focused on the varied meanings and definitions of narrative. The histories of narrative are embedded in particular disciplines and therefore attract separate as well as multiple meanings. This starting point makes it difficult to agree a precise definition. Amidst these tensions, questions arise about where we look for stories and more specifically whether television programs, interviews, diaries, photographs, to name a few possibilities, should be ready sources for this kind of project (Andrews et al., 2013). All of this discussion has led to confusion and contradictory discussions about storytelling and self-inquiry as instruments of investigation.

Several authors have suggested that narrative research is still an evolving field of study and it will be some time before a clear account of narrative research comes to light (Lyons, 2010). Nevertheless, narrative seems to hold such promise because it captures the complexity and fullness of lived experiences, in the past and present, including creative expressions offering a deeper understanding of our social world. The work of Bruner (2004) in 'Life as Narrative' suggests narrative as a distinct form of knowledge which is organized through stories people talk about as vital to making sense of the world. This form of thought relies on narrative as a means of constructing ourselves in our past, present and future lives by the roles we play as stories continue to unfold. Bruner (2004) frames his ideas about narrative from a social constructionist perspective, pointing to constructed accounts in life events and social interaction with others. Taking this idea further, Brand (2015: 517) points out that 'if life is lived through stories we tell, then it must also potentially allow individuals to adapt, shift and modify their stories, transforming their lived experiences. This goes to the very heart of the power of the story, a vehicle with the potential to (re)order, (re) structure, and (re)direct one's life in more meaningful and integrated ways.'

The appeal of narrative research for social work is its attention not just to lived experiences in local, social and cultural contexts but also counter-metanarratives, images of the preconceptions and myths used to maintain gendered and racial inequalities. This significance of experiential knowledge is critical to lines of inquiry about links to larger systems of power, dominance and inequity (Baines, 2002). This narrative and storytelling approach serves to value the social context framing practice, bringing people's experience to contribute to theorizing (Williams and Graham, 2016).

Much has been written about more participatory methodologies, which engage people in research as a process of change and in the co-production of research design and knowledge, in the analysis of research outcomes and their uses (Williams and Graham, 2013). In reviewing narrative approaches in research, it was pleasing to find such a wide-ranging set of activities from auto-ethnography, autobiographical data, biographical self-reflection and inquiry, narrative analysis to art, representative con-structions, performance and photo voice. In this next section I move on to explore their connections with reflective practice, critical social work and personal stories.

One such example of this interdisciplinary application is narratives with long-standing traditions in the disciplines of history and literature drawing on personal documents of significant historical figures. This work with narratives took the forms of journals, diaries, personal papers and letters providing insights into what shaped the ideas and experiences of individuals during particular events, times of historical significance or motivations for achievement in individuals' lives. As Lawler (1998: 72) notes, the distinction between these earlier applications of narrative 'is the view that all human meaning making is achieved by and through the use of narratives or stories' and are naturally occurring source materials from people which explain the experiences that affect them. Currently, narrative approaches to research have entered the social sciences, covering a wide range of topic areas, including professions such as social work. Narrative approaches to research bring with them a reframing of relationships between researcher and participant.

Autobiography – narrative and telling your own story

Following the rise in cultural studies, with its emphasis on language and repre-sentation, an 'autobiographical' turn has signaled the prominence of the study of lives in forms of social inquiry. Of course, the popularity of autobiography has a long history stemming from literature and philosophy, where narratives discuss how lives became what they are, drawing together the past in the 'I' of the present (Martin, 1986). In the postmodern era, narrating individual lives has opened up possibilities of new accounts suggesting 'the appeal of biographical research is that it is exploring in diverse methodological and interpretative ways, how individual accounts can be understood within the contemporary and structural settings' (Roberts, 2002: 5).

Autobiographical self-reflection holds an important place in developing skills of self-inquiry to examine one's own practice and self. This blending of self-reflection and narrative is well developed in Johns's (2010) model of structured reflective self-inquiry. He describes narrative inquiry as reflective practice. Moreover, guided reflection as a process of 'narrative can be only known through living and reflecting on it ... narrative, through reflection, nurtures mindfulness. Narrative is mindful practice, mindful research, mindful teaching' (Johns, 2010: 1).

For Johns (2010), the construction of narrative opens up a reflective space in which to reflect and learn. Even though guidelines are helpful, Johns wants to abandon formulas to construct narrative and would rather take a tentative path using a metaphor of a mountaineer feeling her way along the edge, taking care because the terrain is unknown. Breaking away from convention and throwing caution to the wind lends itself to research as something lived and alive – a kind of truth that is finding its own expression. According to Johns (2010), people learn more from narratives than from conventional theory and he argues this is why its importance is elevated in professional practice contexts.

One of the important features of narrative is its application in interdisciplinary connections as researchers recognize shared interest and common issues as well as the benefits of collaboration to define and establish disciplinary fields (Roberts, 2002). This development has taken place with regard to childhood studies where sociologists have employed new approaches to understanding children's lives as well as a reframing of childhood. As these perspectives have gathered pace, research activities across disciplines attempt to integrate knowledge to address adequately the complex and multidimensional aspects of childhood in different ways (Graham, 2011). This interdisciplinary approach has led to the development of childhood studies taking a revised perspective of childhood where attention is paid to the evolving agency of children and their subjective experiences, meaning and content of everyday life from multiple perspectives with direct relevance for social work. This approach accords children the primary unit of study as social persons in their own right, emphasizing children's own voices as most reflective of their selves, their lived experiences and their social realities. The notion of children's voices takes a central place in the social study of childhood, offering new spaces for children to convey their perspectives, bringing a better understanding of their experiences. Interest in children's lives is focused on the here and now as they are lived rather than thinking about children as future adults. What is everyday life like for children in different environments and how do children make sense of their social world?

Opening up these spaces brings together sociology and cultural studies in order to uncover hidden aspects of children's lives.

This area is of particular interest to me as a social work educator teaching students in their work with children across child welfare institutions. My interest considers dominant discourses framing professional practice which are summarized neatly by Alanen (2004): 'children were typically treated as "dependent variables" of various categories, adults, professionals and institutions who "have" children, take care of them, work on them, are responsible for organizing their living conditions, or in any other way relate to them. Consequently, children were looked upon from the viewpoint of adults, professionals, agencies and institutions.' I suggest that these discourses have created deficit models of children, where too much attention is given to the ages and stages of children as future adults, leaving out investigations into what it means to be a child in contemporary society.

It is widely recognized that children experience a multiplicity of childhoods which are diverse, fluid, with socio-cultural factors such as class, ethnicity, gender and disability all having social and material effects on their experiences. As Holland (2008: 6) notes, 'societal expectations of children from particular socio-economic and cultural backgrounds will strongly affect how people respond to children and how these children develop their own sense of self.' These experiences are particularly acute for children in public welfare settings where they are already disadvantaged and their life chances have been limited by factors outside their control. Deeper understanding of their everyday lives has opened up participatory approaches in professional practice with opportunities to hear more children's voices about their experiences and listen to their stories to help to craft practice supporting their emotional and social well-being. It is encouraging to see some key features of narrative research have been introduced into practice through the children's rights agenda, giving voice through participation. Increasingly children are being asked to reflect upon their lives and their opinions are an integral part of regular reviews in public care. These narratives are making important contributions not only to practice but also professional knowledge, bringing broader understanding of their lives, often challenging assumptions, which tend to veer towards 'children with problems' neglecting to include the good things from children themselves. Holland (2008: 19) succinctly advocates for narrative approaches in this way:

> By paying attention to the narratives told by young people we listen to what they choose to tell us, and how they frame themselves and others within the story. This gives some insight into how they see themselves, or at least the 'face' they wish to present to the person they are talking to. It gives some indication of their priorities and how they respond to, replicate or perhaps challenge dominant discourses about, for example, childhoods, gendered identities, performing family, being in care.

Because the notion of children's voices and perspectives occupies a central place in the field of childhood studies, narrative research holds promise pushing through a more integrated approach toward children in context. Researchers in this field are turning to children in public care settings to learn more about their everyday lives and experiences (Sandbaek, 1999; Murray and Hallett, 2000; Thomas and O'Kane, 2000). These perspectives offer possibilities for reshaping practice as we learn more about children's lives. Despite the challenges in research with children as active co-researchers, narrative approaches acknowledge forms of knowing that children share in this world.

Auto-ethnography – self-inquiry

Over the past decade there has been increasing interest in auto-ethnography, a term used to describe personal writing or self-narrative research. Ellis and Bochner (2000: 739) provide a useful picture of auto-ethnography:

> Autobiographical genre of writing and research that displays multiple layers of consciousness, connecting the personal to the cultural. Back and forth auto ethnographers gaze, first through an ethnographic wide-angle lens, focusing outward on social and cultural aspects of the personal experience; then they look inward, exposing a vulnerable self that is moved by and may move through, refract and resist cultural interpretations.

This quotation directs attention to the researcher's story, reflecting upon both experiences within and outside the research context. Researchers engage in reflection and questioning of their own position as well as the lived experience within time and place in the research process overall. This method of narrative research combines personal narrative and reflective practice as a way of thinking about and studying experience. Narrative inquiry takes this reflective path moving in the field, taking starting points in the telling of stories or lived experiences. Clandinin and Huber (2009) identify three common places researchers can study people's lived experiences inside as well as outside the inquiry. First, the area of temporality, meaning directing attention to the past, present and future of people, events and things under study. This because we are always composing and revising our autobiographies as we go along, including a researcher's inquiry into self. Next is sociality, and here personal and social conditions are given attention. Personal conditions relate to feelings, hopes, desires and moral dispositions alongside social conditions that are present as lives and events unfold. On top of these points is the relationship between the researcher and participants themselves as they are closely involved in the research process itself. Finally, the importance of place in the research process, as our identities and experiences are tied to geographical and situated places infused in the stories we tell about our experiences.

Narrative inquiry has attracted some concerns, particularly in relation to emotions and the writing of highly personalized accounts of lived experiences. Ellis is a well-known auto-ethnographer, writing personal accounts of family members and lived experiences including grief and loss. She advocates living the experience of doing research, which involves all aspects of self including our emotional lives as she wrote about the relationship and care of her mother. She writes: 'My biggest fears in writing about my mother while she was alive included hurting her and the changing relational dynamics that might result' (Ellis, 2007: 18).

There is no doubt that articulating the connections between the researcher and the experiences of research in the form of self-inquiry and analysis is growing across many disciplines. This thirst for self-inquiry and artistic expression bringing social sciences and humanities together is gaining momentum. Broussine et al. (2015) argue strongly that emotional and experiential aspects of research have been rendered deviant from the norms of research practice and so are often written out of research accounts. Researchers are sometimes said to have 'gone off track' by supervisors or gatekeepers with a 'mist' surrounding the researcher/ research relationship. Much of the shift towards self-inquiry is grounded in postmodern ideas as well as interest in everyday lives with language and meaning as the backdrop for these trends. Obviously, narrative and human experiences are inextricably connected and narrative attempts to capture a broader picture including life in documents recorded in the form of case studies, diaries, journals and memoirs.

Conclusion

In re-reading this chapter, the general aim has been to sketch out the emerging field of narrative research with reference to its application and possibilities in social work. This is not an easy task since the breadth of approaches covers a wide range of areas including methods drawn from outside the social sciences. In this context, I have just touched the surface of this growing field of inquiry as I become aware of experimental research embracing the visual arts and performance transforming what we understand as 'research' to capture deeper understanding and meanings in human experiences as valuable in their own right. Narrative approaches in research across education, nursing and social work, amongst others, is evident in literature, journals and textbooks creating new ways to understand how others see and experience the world. In learning more about lived experiences it is possible to improve practice in increasingly complex and changing environments. New and changing needs on the practice floor imply flexibility as well as participation and consultation, all of which are embedded in a narrative scheme of thinking and practice. This engagement is closely tied to reflective practice and self-inquiry both as a process and product, encouraging the ongoing need for self-reflection and critical examination of one's own identity and social location. This growing interest draws on narrative to describe and critically examine the experience of research itself, including its researcher's emotional feelings and experiences. In all of this, narrative inquiry infused by postmodern thinking continues to motivate researchers to transcend boundaries and envision new possibilities in research process, methods and outcomes.

References

Alanen, L. (2004) *Theorizing children's welfare*, Paper presented at New Perspectives on Childhood, University of Leeds, UK, 12–14 November.

Andrews, M., Squire, C. and Tamboukou, M. (2013) *Doing narrative research* (2nd edn), London: Sage.

Baines, D. (2002) 'Race, class and gender in the everyday talk of social workers: the ways we limit the possibilities for radical practice,' *Race, Gender and Class Journal*, 9(1): 145–167.

Barnes, M. (2006) *Caring and social justice*, Basingstoke: Palgrave Macmillan.

Beauboeuf-Lafontant, T. (2007) '"You have to show strength": an exploration of gender, race and depression,' *Gender and Society*, 21(1): 28–51.

Bowpitt, G. (1998) 'Evangelical, Christianity, secular humanism, and the genesis of British social work,' *British Journal of Social Work*, 28(5): 675–693.

Brand, G. (2015) 'Through the looking glass space of new ways of knowing: a personal research narrative,' *The Qualitative Report*, 20(4): 516–525.

Brew, A. (1998) 'Moving beyond paradigm boundaries.' In J. Higgs (ed.), *Writing qualitative research*, Sydney, Australia: Hampden Press, pp. 29–48.

Broussine, M., Watts, L. and Clarke, C. (2015) 'Why should researchers be interested in their feelings.' In C. Clarke, M. Broussine and L. Watts (eds), *Researching with feeling, the emotional aspects of social and organizational research*, London: Routledge.

Bruner, J. (2004) 'Life as narrative,' *Social Research: An International Quarterly*, 7(3): 691–710.

Bryant, L. (2015) *Critical and creative research: methodologies in social work*, Aldershot: Ashgate.

Cihodariu, M. (2012) 'Narratives as instrumental research and as attempts of fixing meaning the uses and misuses of the concept "narratives",' *Journal of Comparative Research in Anthropology and Sociology*, 3(2): 27–43.

Clandinin, D.J. and Huber, J. (2009) 'Narrative inquiry.' In B. McGaw, E. Baker and P.P. Peterson (eds), *International encyclopedia of education* (3rd edn), New York, NY: Elsevier.

Clarke, C., Broussine, M. and Watts, L. (2015) *Researching with feeling, the emotional aspects of social and organizational research*, London: Routledge.

Coble, A. (2006) *Cleaning up: the transformation of domestic service in 20th century New York City*, New York: Routledge.

Denzin, N. and Lincoln, Y. (2011) *The Sage handbook of qualitative research*, Thousand Oaks: Sage.

Ellis, C. (2007) 'Telling secrets, revealing lives: relational ethics in research with intimate others,' *Qualitative Inquiry*, 13(1): 3–29.

Ellis, C. and Bochner, A. (2000) 'Autoethnography, personal narrative, reflexivity: researcher as subject.' In N. Denzin and Y. Lincoln (eds), *The handbook of qualitative research*, Thousand Oaks: Sage, pp. 733–768.

Falconer, E. (2009) 'Telling tales: a feminist interpretation of women's travel narratives,' *Enquire*, 3: 21–40.

Fine, M. (2007) *A caring society?* Basingstoke: Palgrave Macmillan.

Finlay, L. (2002) '"Outing the researcher": the provenance, process, and practice of reflexivity,' *Qualitative Health Research*, 12(4): 531–545.

Freire, P. (1972) *Pedagogy of the oppressed*, Harmondsworth: Penguin.

Gilgun, J.F. and Abrams, S. (2002) 'The nature and usefulness of qualitative social work research,' *Qualitative Social Work*, 1(1): 39–55.

Gordon, G. (2001) 'Transforming lives: towards bicultural competence.' In P. Reason and H. Bradbury (eds), *Handbook of action research*, Thousand Oaks: Sage, pp. 314–323.

Gordon, G. (2007) *Towards bi-cultural competence*, Staffordshire, UK: Trentham Books.

Graham, M. (2007) 'The ethics of care. Black women and the social professions: implications of a new analysis,' *Ethics and Social Welfare*, 1(2): 176–194.

Graham, M. (2011) 'Changing conditions and paradigms of childhood: implications for the social professions and social work,' *British Journal of Social Work*, 41(8): 1532–1547.

Higgs, J. and Cant, R. (1998) 'What is qualitative research.' In J. Higgs (ed.), *Writing qualitative research*, New South Wales, Australia: Hampden Press.

Higgs, J. and Llewellyn, G. (1998) 'Framing the research questions.' In J. Higgs (ed.), *Writing qualitative research*, New South Wales, Australia: Hampden Press.

Hill-Collins, P. (2000) *Black feminist thought: knowledge, consciousness and the politics of empowerment* (2nd edn), London: Routledge.

Holland, S. (2008) 'The everyday lives of children in care using sociological perspectives to inform social work practice,' *Working paper* qualiti/WPS/005 ESRC, Cardiff University.

Humphries, B. (2008) *Social work research for social justice*, Basingstoke: Palgrave Macmillan.

Hunter, T. (1998) *To joy to freedom: southern black women's lives and labor after the Civil War*, Massachusetts: Harvard University Press.

Johns, C. (2010) *Guided reflection: a narrative approach to advancing professional practice*, Oxford: Wiley.

Lawler, J. (1998) 'Adapting a phenomenological philosophy to research and writing.' In J. Higgs (ed.), *Writing qualitative research*, New South Wales, Australia: Hampden Press.

Lorde, A. (1984) *Sister outsider*, New York: The Crossing Press.

Lorenz, W. (2011) 'Research as an element in social work's ongoing search for identity.' In V. Cree (ed.), *Social work: a reader*, London: Routledge, pp. 48–57.

Lyons, N. (2010) *Handbook of reflection and reflective inquiry*, New York: Springer.

Margolis, H. (1993) *Paradigms and barriers: how habits of mind govern scientific beliefs*, Chicago: University of Chicago Press.

Martin, W. (1986) *Recent theories of narrative*, Ithaca, NY: Cornell University Press.

McAdams, D. (1993) *The stories we live by: personal myths and the making of self*, New York: W. Morrow.

McDonald, C. (2006) *Challenging social work: the context of practice*, London: Palgrave.

Murray, C. and Hallett, C. (2000) 'Young people's participation in decisions affecting their welfare,' *Childhood: a Global Journal of Child Research*, 7(1): 11–25.

Noble, D. (2005) 'Remembering bodies, healing histories: the emotional politics of everyday freedom.' In C. Alexander and C. Knowles (eds), *Making race matter, bodies, space and identity*, Basingstoke: Palgrave, pp. 132–152.

Pickering, M. (2008) *Research methods for cultural studies*, Edinburgh: Edinburgh University Press.

Plummer, K. (1995a) 'Telling sexual stories in a late modern world,' *Studies in Symbolic Interactionism*, 18: 101–120.

Plummer, K. (1995b) *Telling sexual stories, power change and social worlds*, London: Routledge.

Reissman, C.K. (1994) 'Making sense of marital violence.' In C.K. Riessman (ed.), *Qualitative studies in social work research*, Thousand Oaks: Sage.

Reissman, C.K. (2012) 'Analysis of personal narratives.' In R. Miller, L. Reid, W. James and A. Fortune, *Qualitative research in social work*, New York: Columbia University Press.

Roberts, B. (2002) *Biographical research*, Buckingham: Open University.

Ryan, A. (2001) *Feminist ways of knowing*, Leicester: National Institute of Adult Continuing Education.

Sandbaek, M. (1999) 'Children with problems: focusing on everyday life,' *Children and Society*, 13: 106–118.

Shaw, I. and Gould, N. (2001) *Qualitative research in social work*, London: Sage.

Thomas, N. and O'Kane, C. (2000) 'Discovering what children think: connections between research and practice,' *British Journal of Social Work*, 30(6): 810–835.

Tronto, J. (1993) *Moral boundaries: a political argument for an ethnic of care*, New York: Routledge.

Weick, A. (1993) 'Reconstructing social work education,' *Journal of Teaching in Social Work*, 8(1/2): 11–30.

Williams, C. and Graham, M. (2013) *Social work in Europe*, London: Routledge.

Williams, C. and Graham, M. (2016) *Social work in a diverse society*, Bristol: Policy Press.

PART II

Student narratives

INTRODUCING STUDENT NARRATIVES

Social work is acknowledged to be a value-based profession steeped in moral purpose, shaping its character in acts of professional service. Notably, definitions of social work continue to be debated and are evolving in part because of the wide-ranging tasks undertaken by social workers across different countries according to different welfare systems. In many countries definitions of social work are broader, taking in community-orientated activities and an integral part of daily practice (Cree, 2011). In 2014, international social work organizations the International Federation of Social Workers (IFSW) and the International Association of Schools of Social Work (IASSW) agreed upon the following definition:

> Social work is a practice-based profession and an academic discipline that promotes social change and development, social cohesion, and the empowerment and liberation of people. Principles of social justice, human rights, collective responsibility and respect for diversities are central to social work. Underpinned by theories of social work, social sciences, humanities and indigenous knowledge, social work engages people and structures to address life challenges and enhance wellbeing.
>
> *(IFSW, 2014)*

These values express social work commitments to social change and development, latching on to moral priorities of social justice and human rights issues. This grounding builds on diverse approaches to professional caring practice in social work, which appeals to people thinking about a career in social work. In this context LeCroy (2002: 2) uses the term 'the call to social work,' as he believes many people are called to do social work, observing that 'their efforts are to contribute to compassion and justice in the world, to pursue social transformations, to provide a vision for a better way of living. Their day-to-day work is encircled by compassionate treatment of others. Because of their calling most of them have immense hearts and deep souls.'

Of course, there are varied, complex and changing motivations among students entering the social work profession, yet there are common themes including wanting to make a difference in people's lives. In a study by Furness (2007: 248) quotes from students provide some examples of these ambitions: 'working with people to achieve growth and change,' helping others to help themselves; 'enabling people to reach their full potential,' filtering into social work as a challenging and rewarding career. Alongside these individual and personalized contributions as social workers, there is an overarching appeal of the profession's commitment to social change and development linked with issues of inequality, oppression and care of vulnerable populations.

In his book, *The Call to Social Work*, LeCroy (2002) presents life stories from social workers in the field – narrative descriptions about the work and professional lives of social workers. He rightly acknowledges the lack of literature to capture the day-to-day lives of social workers, arguing that if we had these data of practice over time we would be able to examine the ways in which practice has developed. When I began to think about writing a book about reflection, critical theory and student narratives, I found many books about reflective practice, sometimes including a step-by-step approach to writing and other reflective activities. On the other hand, there are few books that document the stories of students themselves as they move through social work education to become practitioners. This chapter throws some light on students' motivations, hopes and fears as they enter the social work profession. They write about their life experiences and how these experiences have influenced their decisions to become social workers. When I sent out a call for student narratives, I asked students to consider their personal stories and life experiences and how these elements shaped their motivations and practice. I also asked about their identities and the ways in which they understood themselves through this lens to the world. Importantly, as Christie and Weeks (1998: 56) point out, 'life stories are created, sustained, re-worked and drawn upon by social work students and social workers have implications for their education and practice.' These authors argue that life experience is a neglected form of knowledge in education and practice. Everyday encounters in practice bring together professional and personal worlds which can evoke a sense of needing to understand self and know more – a kind of own knowing in the context of care giving and social relationships.

As I read and reviewed the student narratives in this section of the book, I was reminded of the variations and local contexts of social work across the world. The lives of students are embedded in the social, cultural and political relations of their society. Both Payne (2005) and Dominelli (2009) provide a useful if not simplistic way of defining these diverse roles, including therapeutic, transformational, maintenance and emancipatory representing social work activities connecting across and with each other. Transformational and emancipatory approaches associated with collective-based and community responses. While these diverse roles continue to be at the center of ongoing debates about social work commitments to social justice issues versus maintaining the status quo in crafting practice methods, social work's professional standing and role across the world is complex despite calls to universalize the profession. Alongside these diverse activities are a range of social work cultures across the world. By this I am referring to the professional cultures of social work, including education, which have taken up common hallmarks of the profession yet are bound by their own histories of social work, socioeconomic, cultural, development, political and educational pathways. This complicated mix filters into students' experiences of internship or field placement activities as they move through the process of social work education. The following narratives are full of learning stories that illuminate the importance of human experience and meaning. They convey a patchwork of experiences, feelings and emotions all coming together with personal stories to reveal a more complete view of student journeys through education and into professional practice. Some of the narratives are brief and sketchy while others are longer and more detailed, and include views and perspectives about a wide range of issues. This reflective space captures student narratives, moving along the primary themes of identities, outsider perspectives, social justice, empowerment, child welfare, and journeys through social work education.

As I wrote the introductions to each narrative, I resisted the temptation to analyze and present my appreciative reading of the narratives. Instead, I wanted to leave space for others to do their own reading and make their own interpretations in order to keep in mind the power of narratives as learning stories. Stories presented here also invite questions about how their stories are narrated. How do the students position themselves and in what ways do they interpret the meaning and significance of their experiences? The narratives invite readers to find a space, sit back and discover more about their own experiences as they engage in an ongoing dialogue with narratives revealing the interweaving of personal and professional selves. In this way the reader is invited to connect and relate to these narratives themselves. By opening up spaces to reflect and consider their own personal stories, links and connections can be made to think about what we know and how we know it.

As an aside, I want to remind readers that the value in these narratives is precisely because they are not pristine; they still have their rough edges. It is easy in academic environments to look at what is wrong with them and focus on their faults and missing pieces. Rather, they are what they are, and I encourage readers to be open to their positive potential and meanings. Of course, each one is open to many interpretations as every reader will read the narratives differently, according to their own values, interests, experiences and worldviews. One of the good things about narrative is its range of forms and styles for discovering meaning and communication to readers through stories (Peters, 2010). Vanessa starts this collection of narratives with an emphasis on evolving identities. In this dynamic, identities are both a matter of 'becoming' as well as constructed in relation to others and embedded in our cultures, which are fluid and characterized by social change.

References

Christie, A. and Weeks, J. (1998) 'Life experiences: a neglected form of knowledge in social work education and practice,' *Practice*, 10(1): 55–69.

Cree, V. (2011) 'Introduction: reading social work.' In V. Cree (ed.), *Social work: a reader*, Abingdon: Routledge.

Dominelli, L. (2009) *Introducing social work*, Cambridge: Polity Press.

Furness, S. (2007) 'An enquiry into students' motivations to train as social workers in England,' *Journal of Social Work*, 7(2): 239–253.

International Federation of Social Workers (IFSW) (2014) 'Global definition of social work,' available at http://ifsw.org/policies/definition-of-social-work/ (accessed 16 December 2015).

LeCroy, C. (2002) *The call to social work: life stories*, Thousand Oaks, CA: Sage.

Payne, M. (2005) *Modern social work theory* (3rd edn), Chicago: Lyceum Books.

Peters, S. (2010). *Democracy and higher education: traditions and stories of civic engagement*, East Lansing: Michigan State University Press.

4

THE VOICE OF MY JOURNEY (VANESSA CORREA)

PROFILE

Vanessa Correa identifies as a Chicana/Mexican-American mujerista, born in the County of Los Angeles, CA. She received her BA in Chicana/Latina Studies and Psychology at California State University, Long Beach. She is passionate about social justice and equity within the field of community mental health. She is a cultural enthusiast, and enjoys building a collective consciousness within the Latina com-*munity. She is currently a candidate for a Master's in Social Work at California State University, Dominguez Hills, and class of 2016.*

Introduction

In the first narrative, Vanessa introduces herself as a Chicana, Mexican-American woman and tells her story through her decision to become a social worker and study the field of theory and practice. She is motivated by her passion for social justice in the practice area of community mental health. Vanessa tells us about her early life and how these experiences have shaped and continue to influence her identity. Vanessa reflects upon her evolving identity, describing the ambiguities and complexities as she pieces together intersections of class, ethnicity, cultural consciousness, family background, social location, environment and social conditions in the wider society. As her short story reveals, these elements seemed to create tensions, yet there were driving forces and some luck which moved her towards higher education, fuelling her desire to enter graduate work in this field.

★★★

> Like others having or living in more than one culture, we get multiple, often opposing messages. The coming together of two self-consistent but habitually incomparable frames of reference causes un choque, a cultural collision.
>
> *(Anzaldua, 1987: 78)*

This excerpt from the distinguished Chicana feminist theorist, scholar and political poet Gloria Anzaldua, in her work *Borderlands/La Frontera: The New Mestiza*, resonates with my lived experiences through my development within the personal, educational and professional settings; a trajectory that yielded my conscious decision for entering the field of Social Work. The development of my identity as a fusion of intrapsychic, interpersonal and societal exchanges has led me to this current stance of social service and what envelopes the role of a helper. My subjectivity as a woman of color, whose roots are entrenched within the collectivistic Latina heritage that is of my parents and ancestral lineage, meshed within the individualistic US culture that my physical birth has me bounded to a whirlwind of positives and negatives, underscoring the tumultuous relations between the privileges and disadvantages that have manifested in my life. These oppositional realities and experiences are what have molded me into who I am today, succeeding my existential passion for furthering my knowledge and entering the realm of social work.

Being my primary agent of socialization, my family premised my values, beliefs, customs and traditions manifesting themselves in my thoughts, feelings, perspectives and actions. I grew up in a lower middle class, bilingual Spanish and English, Latina household wherein both parents are first generation migrants from Mexico, blue collar laborers, and of fervent practice of the Catholic faith.

I am the youngest of two children, and being female, I was kept at an even closer proximity to the family as the gender role expectations were enforced – my every action and comportment dictated within social constructs of what it is to be female, and enforced by my family and social institutions. I felt I was always kept at arms' length. Consequently, I grew very attached to my family – I limited my interactions in social settings, always yearning for the sensation of being enclosed within the comfort of my home.

The neighborhood I grew up in was of middle class families, majority being of Filipino heritage. It was a safe and quiet environment. The culture within the neighborhood was very individualistic with a pretentious outlook. My parents are tenacious laborers, sacrificing even that which they did not have, pushing beyond their physical and mental limits to provide for their children, and their parents. My parents were the first in their families to own a home, obtain a steady income, health care, and own an automobile. They were of humble and modest living.

Being the first to permeate through the middle class level, my parents faced great challenges. I witnessed the struggles to maintain this status. My parents are both strong-willed people who strive for better living conditions. They underwent a strenuous process navigating through a system that garners anti-immigrant rhetoric. Their transnational experiences and impoverished upbringing taught them to be resourceful, frugal and give to others who did not have the means. Their narratives and social modeling ignited within me the flame of determination to excel in life, understand the importance of human relationships, be of service to others, and seek justice for those who are being excluded from attaining the basic human necessities pertinent for a quality life.

In ensuring a great educational experience, my parents enrolled my brother and I in private Catholic education. It was a small student body, one of upper middle class, majority being of Filipino decent. My menial middle class status was very apparent and translated through my physical appearance and speech, albeit the uniform attire that was mandatory for all students. I did not obtain concepts of materials, types of knowledge and understandings that majority of my classmates knew of, such as the latest technology, studying habits, and various resources that facilitated their success within the private school setting. Schoolmates that I engaged with were of the Filipino culture. Often I felt ostracized. I did not look like them. I did not speak Tagalog as they did. I did not know or understand their cultural traditions when they shared their family stories and outings. Even when they referenced the popular culture, I felt I couldn't contribute as my social development was delayed, and the only female I could relate to was my Mexican mother.

There was a scarcity of Latina representation in the school. My parents felt the importance of making the household monolingual English, so as to avoid 'confusion' for my brother and I in our studies and educational advancement in school. They stopped speaking to me in Spanish and I began to lose my linguistic ability. Latina media of television and radio allowed me to maintain knowledge and understanding of the Spanish language and validated my Latina culture, along with family gatherings, holiday traditions and home cooking. But amongst my peers, I was withdrawn from my heritage – to the extent that I felt ashamed of it. I developed a split per-sonality where I disowned my Latina culture in school amongst my peers and teachers, but regained allegiance inside my house and with extended family.

I felt my religion further suppressed my inner desires, and controlled my behaviors. I was taught to mimic the 'infallible' actions of the saints and, specifically, mirror the Virgin Mary as obedient, enduring, self-sacrificing, humble and chaste. I was molded to perceive that my value was limited to how well I pleased authority figures, followed God's commandments, and maintaining the sanctity of sexual abstinence. Moments I did not follow these rigid standards, immense guilt succeeded. The shame that my actions and thoughts were grave sins made me think I was culpable for all my shortcomings. I developed a low self-esteem, and low con-fidence. I felt in limbo: yearning to belong, but couldn't make connections. I was disconnected from social groups, isolated from my peers. It was very daunting: the foreign individualistic US culture, the upper middle class customs that did not fit my socioeconomic status, and the religious ideals. As Anzaldua states in her auto-biography, 'The ambivalence from the clash of voices results in mental and emotional states of perplexity … The mestiza's dual or multiple personality is plagued by psychic restlessness.' I related too well to this excerpt (Anzaldua, 1987: 78). I was wavering within multiple institutions that were restraining and dissuading me from self-expression, all the while feeling more disconnected from the symbol that brought me a sense of comfort: my Mexican roots. The one thing I felt in control was my education and efforts to move up the learning ladder. The echo of my mother's voice engrained in my psyche: 'You are going to be something great in life. Get an education, get a career; so that you will not have to struggle and sacrifice so much as your father and I have for so many years.' I made that my central focus. I did not understand at the moment that I was processing and struggling with the process of acculturation – I was assimilating, slowly demarcating my ethnic roots, and restricting the multidimensional capability of my identity formation.

At the conclusion of those nine years in private school, I developed a desire to reclaim my Mexican culture. A form of cultural resistance and reconciliation slowly ensued. The public high school I attended was majority composed of Caucasian and Asian students, geographically located in a middle class city. Starting at a new environment, I was determined to reconnect with my ethnic heritage, solidify my cultural bonds and make more concrete what is part of my physical, emotional, and spiritual make-up. I chose to take up the Spanish language course to enhance my skills and connection to being a Latina. The minute discourse of culture in this class kept my soul satiated. I also enrolled myself in a Mexican folk dance group outside of school in a nearby city. I made my debut in my newly claimed identity at my Quinceañera [15th birthday] fully immersed in the cultural practices and customs. I felt my self-esteem increasing as my thoughts and behaviors began harmonizing. In this process I began making connections with the few Latina students present. I bonded with them, and grew enamored with the idea that they demonstrated a shared reality as my familial upbringing: they knew about novelas, family traditions of foods and authentic dishes, rock en español, Mexican proverbs and idioms that were humorous, and what it is to synergistically speak the two languages and create Spanglish. Their expressions were embellished with the idiosyncrasy of what it is to be a first generation child of Mexican parents living in the US. The integration of the Mexican culture with the US culture: the creation of a Mexican-American way of life. This is when I conscientiously proclaimed myself a Chicana. I was proud of my Mexican heritage, and aware of popular US culture: understanding the hybridity that collided in what is my social make-up.

As I was growing awareness of who I was internally, my social attunement increased; I was also becoming conscientious of how others viewed me, my friends, and others of the Latina race. I started taking note of the discriminations and social differences that existed between people of my race and other ethnicities in the school. I had a lot of questions in my mind. I observed the disproportional rates of Latina students who would begin the school year, and within one month 'transferred' to a continuation school. It was almost as if they were 'deported,' coerced, and displaced to an isolated setting, transmitting the message that they were deficient, and unequipped for forming part of the student body. Some of my family members were subjected to this maltreatment. I knew I was part of the minority in my school. Those who remained were considered to be 'highly dedicated' to their educational aptitude. I continued to assume the role of a tenacious student who excelled in all classes – as if I was also internalizing these slanderous insinuations associating Latina students as 'unskilled,' and 'unintelligent.' I figured as long as I could be a 'grade A' student, I will be worthy and I will be respected despite my allegiance to my Latinidad [Latin-ness]. I was learning the ideal of meritocracy. And so I integrated this aspect into my identity – ascribing my self-worth on my educational achievements.

However, I felt my efforts were kept unchallenged and did not supersede my potential. Neither teachers nor academic counselors provided me with additional resources, let alone held conversations that would benefit me in attaining a higher education post-high school. There were no discussions of the process or steps to embark on to identify what professional career I wanted in life. It was not until I had a mandatory session with my academic counselor that it became clear to me; this lack of regard was more than likely associated with my racial and gender identities. It was a brief meeting. It was my junior year, and my progress in school was in discussion. He glanced at my grades, and stated in a shocked tone, 'Well, you are doing exceptionally well for someone like you. That's great. You've got nothing to worry about. Just keep it up, and soon you'll be graduated.' I could not get one sentence through before he sent me away. I was ignored, and dismissed. My grades were a success on their own – no further discourse of post-graduation plans was needed.

I resorted to inquiring about the college application process on my own with the help of my mom – two inexperienced individuals navigating yet another foreign system. I learned as I came across terms such as student tuition, scholarships, grants, etc. I did not know anything about the college culture; it was a hard learning curve that I directly was faced with, meanwhile my parents vicariously living it. My college career uncovered a multitude of perspectives and ideologies that brought me familiarity and ambivalence. I felt in the crossroads again. I knew I wanted to study human behavior – how the discipline of psychology could offer my curiosity of learning 'what it is we do' and 'why we do it.' However, I was captivated with the discipline that encapsulated my entire being: Chicana/Latina Studies. I had come across an area of scholarship that validated my lived experiences and that of my family. I was addicted to the literature. I grew an affinity for social and ethnic narratives. I was growing a higher understanding, a more astute way of critiquing social events, with a foundation of historical accounts to make sense of it all. I developed a critical lens on my surroundings. I was trained to question everything that I was indoctrinated to accept as 'truth.' I started the process of de-colonization – I started defacing the multifaceted ideologies that for my lifetime had suppressed me, and led me to believe it was my place.

I was undoing racial stigmas and biases that I held about my own community and against myself: the lazy, drunk, gang banging Latino male; the sexual, promiscuous Latina, or the Latina who is devalued for her domestic labor skills. I realized how the mainstream culture creates and molds these false archetypes and claims them as 'truths,' consequently shaping the social, political, and economic barriers for Latinas to succeed in life. I could not walk away from this new discovery. It was a difficult transformation to undergo; concurrently, it was an empowering one to shed these dehumanizing labels. Once knowledge is learned, it cannot be reversed. And I could no longer ignore the social decay that was affecting those of my racial group, and other racial groups who have been historically marginalized and placed in the peripheries of society. It became a personal need for me to address these inequalities, empower my community and in the process reinforce my autonomy from the restraints of degrading societal constructs.

This collective consciousness was the catalyst of merging my fascination of human behavior and service to my cultural Latina community. The historical and present racial discriminations and social disparities experienced by Latinas, and its consequence of internalized oppression, produce a vicious infrastructure of violence, trauma and control which is pervasive throughout an individual's intrapsychic, interpersonal and social functioning. These issues invigorate my motivation to advocate, educate, deconstruct, reconstruct, train, coach, collaborate, explore, critically analyze and empower racial minorities and others who have been disenfranchised within the community mental health structure. It was then that I knew my professional career belongs to the field of social work.

Presently striving for my social work master's degree, I take note of my journey of self-awareness: past and present. I am cognizant of the importance of reflective learning – the strengths, and areas of improvements that it yields. Self-reflecting allows to assess and re-assess one's own abilities, perceptions and skills. I realize that this process of self-reflection exists on a continuum and is evolutionary. It has allowed me to see how my past has been influenced by current positions, attitudes and perceptions as well as looking onwards in changing certain behaviors or outlooks that will help me become a better social worker and service my community with efficiency, competence, and humility. It has allowed me to face myself in the mirror, accept my faults, reconfigure the shortcomings, and rejoice in my successes. I am becoming receptive to the concept that I am a life long learner in the professional and personal realms, concurrently embracing my vulnerability in this process.

Utilizing the lens of critical race theory and intersectionality as paradigms to guide my social work practice in the clinical setting gives me the satisfaction of assessing for more than just 'cultural competency' where the rhetoric of 'diversity' can be misused as a term to deny the reality of racialization and racial oppression in our society and its detrimental consequences on communities of color. I want to be able to provide effective methods of treatment by exploring the inherent strengths embodied by cultural traditions, values and beliefs that are often disregarded or cast as unconventional to western standards. These theoretical modalities engender my self-awareness of biases, power relations, how I perceive myself and of other groups – forcing me to unlearn stigmas and stereotypes that slander particular racial groups, and build new concepts that reclaim positive, more accurate representations.

I stand here today, aware of the disparities across racial groups, socioeconomic status, gender, sexual orientation, ability, age, nationalism, and other social categories that separate the populace, stratifying and enforcing inequity. Intersectionality asserts that our identities comprise of variable interconnected social subgroups by which we hold positions of privilege and oppression alike. I am a young adult, educated, middle class, spiritual, Chicana woman who identifies as a social agitator and a peace maker; a person of knowledge and one who is constantly learning new information; one who takes the lead and also follows. I have discovered the flexibility that I can maneuver through these social labels. I learned to accept my identity as not one-dimensional, but multifaceted. In a society where one must choose one side of a binary position, I refused to conform to only one way of being. I have a tolerance for ambiguity, and nothing is a dichotomous playing field.

> In perceiving conflicting information and points of view, she is subjected to a swamping of her psychological borders. She has discovered that she can't hold concepts or ideas in rigid boundaries ... only by remaining flexible is she able to stretch the psyche horizontally and vertically ... toward a more whole perspective, one that includes rather than excludes.
>
> *(Anzaldua, 1987: 79)*

Like a kaleidoscope, my identity does not have a finite positionality, for the only thing that is constant is change. It is a lifestyle that is not easy to practice, but one that is liberating in its essence. And this helps me continue on my journey as a role of a helper in the field of social work.

References

Anazaldua, G. (1987) *Borderlands/la frontera: the new mestiza*, San Francisco: Aunt Lute Books.

5

REFLECTING CRITICALLY ON MY JOURNEY THROUGH SOCIAL WORK EDUCATION IN AN AUSTRALIAN UNIVERSITY (TEJASWINI PATIL AND MICHELLE MOSS)

PROFILE

Dr Tejaswini Patil is Lecturer at Federation University, Ballarat, Australia. Her research specialization is discourse analysis, reflective practice in social work education, identity and racialized politics in social work. She also has published papers recently on reflective practice in social work education and a discourse analysis of media representations of Muslims in Australia.

Dr Michelle Moss completed her PhD, which explores identity issues for Indigenous children in foster care. Michelle is a qualified Art Therapist who has worked with traumatized children and families in New South Wales, Queensland and the Northern Territory. She has extensive experience as a practitioner in child protection and as a lecturer.

Introduction

Following the first narrative, Tejaswini writing in her own voice acknowledges that her journey, including dialogue, critical feedback and discussion, was only possible through collaboration with her field supervisor, Michelle. Although her narrative is tied to personal experiences, her story moves beyond these elements to encompass the social and the ways in which cultures provide maps of meaning. This act of telling considers her current location in Australia where she describes the process of othering as she finds herself critiquing dominant social work models of practice. Tejaswini develops a deeper awareness of contexts and environments she now occupies, navigating differences in language and cultural practices. The narrative takes the reader through an unraveling self-study where these social constructions of difference seem to sit comfortably in her current dynamic. Then she relates this experience to a nagging contradiction seeping into her own motivations and the intersections of the author's upbringing and background in India. As she reflects on her majority status in India, the process of othering takes another turn as gaze is channeled towards self, not only acknowledging her privileged background but also the dynamics of othering in a location where 'it was important to know who the other was.' Even though we may have our own take on these meanings and how we make sense of them, migration across nations in personal and professional contexts can bring these habits of being in the world to the surface in various ways.

★★★

I reflect on my journey through social work education by discussing how critical reflective learning is central to making connections between personal histories and the developing professional self. In analyzing this connection, I start by providing a brief background as to why I chose to study social work and the subsequent influence of social location and its impact on key aspects of my identity. In exploring how social location intersects with key aspects of my identity, I will reflect on how my awareness of 'self' has shaped and crafted the way I think about social work practice. While the reflection is written in my voice, the recognition and/or engagement with my developing professional identity was a joint collaboration with my field supervisor. This project wouldn't have been possible without the critically reflective feedback, dialogue and discussion that happened through the final placement. Furthermore, the main aim of the reflection was that the supervisory voice added to, rather than distracted from the student narrative, which necessarily is at the forefront.

Brief background to the choice of social work degree

I enrolled in the qualifying Master of Social Work program at one of the universities in Australia after having completed my doctoral studies in sociology at the University of South Australia. In my doctoral studies, I analyzed how discourses of othering were employed to disguise racialized attitudes towards Muslims in Australia and India. Whilst the completion of the doctoral studies was an important professional achievement, I felt uneasy and unsatisfied. After months of reflection it occurred to me that as an international postgraduate student studying for a doctoral degree in Australia, I felt keenly the intersections of race, gender and nationalism.

My position in Australia as a non-white woman with English as a second language paradoxically intersected with reflecting on my positionality as a Hindu middle class woman and my participation in the Hindu majoritarian discourse of Muslim othering. Whilst being away from my country of birth provided me a sense of comfort in reflecting on how discourses of Hindu majoritarianism are reflected in the Hindu–Muslim riots, it also starkly emphasized the fraught nature of being looked at as 'different' and 'not being part of mainstream society.' This realization of the fraught nature of 'lived experiences' and the intractable links between discourse, power and race only clarified in my mind that I had to choose a profession which allowed for the integration and/or exploration of critical reflection of one's 'self' and the way it impacts on the way one views, interprets and embodies it in their practice.

Moving from Adelaide, South Australia to Darwin, Northern Territory

At the beginning of my degree, I was based in Adelaide, South Australia but moved to the Northern Territory and completed the majority of the degree studying externally. Whilst I moved to Darwin to pursue employment, the differences with Adelaide in terms of the public space and the environment were quite noticeable. Darwin, due to its recent colonization by European settlers in the late nineteenth century, remoteness from the rest of Australia, coupled with its closeness to Asia had the feel of what researchers call a 'frontier identity' (Ennis et al., 2014). Its small population of 127,532 in 2010 (Australian Bureau of Statistics, 2011) included 20 percent who were born overseas and 11 percent Indigenous (Ennis et al., 2013). Studies (Carson et al., 2011; Taylor et al., 2014) indicate that cities with a frontier identity such as Darwin have high population turnovers and experience difficulty attracting and retaining skilled workers. Furthermore, Taylor et al. (2014) indicate that Darwin is characterized by greater cultural diversity and high male-to-female ratios. These stark differences in the social and geographical context between Adelaide and Darwin made me feel comfortable.

As I progressed through social work units in the course, I started to notice that most of the reflective pieces I wrote were about how social location impacted on my understanding of my own positionality. While I was in Adelaide, I could feel the uneasiness of my positionality as a non-white woman more intensely, whereas in Darwin I started to recognize, address and discuss these anxieties of living in a western context much more freely through my writing. My writing focused on making connections between place, social context and my own 'self-awareness.' It was filled with analysis and critique of the dominant western paradigm of social work and the way it impacted on people and/or communities from diverse cultural backgrounds.

My observations of everyday social interactions and relationships emphasized the stark differences between dominant western frames and culturally diverse individuals/groups and communities. I acquainted myself with literature on culturally diverse groups in a remote context and developed critiques using Foucauldian theory. The main basis of my critique was the philosophical and moral underpinnings of western social work. Most of these reflective pieces I wrote provided me a platform to connect the complexities of my lived experience with the fraught nature of social and economic disadvantage I noticed in the public sphere in Darwin. I could see a pattern emerging in my thinking: I was using my anxieties as a non-white naturalized Australian woman to position myself as the 'other' and critique the dominant western models of social work, whilst at the same time assuming the role of speaking on behalf of people from diverse cultural backgrounds.

Nearly nine months into my stay in Darwin and the progress through social work education, I was starting to feel comfortable that I was finally able to channel my anxieties about my own positionality using social work theories and pedagogical tools for reflective practice. This comfort zone was ruptured during the early phase of my first field placement, which was a research placement working on a specific research project that didn't involve any direct client contact and/or interaction.[1] During a routine discussion with my field supervisor I mentioned I was starting to notice a pattern in the way people were talking about 'Indigenous people,' 'their culture' and 'need to become more culturally aware of Indigenous history and culture.' My field supervisor asked me to reflect on this observation by examining what made me notice it, why did it upset me, what values and assumptions did I bring to the observation.

Reflecting on this critical incident, I followed the usual pattern, explained my anxieties, positioned myself as the other and developed a discourse critique of social work profession and its code of ethics. I felt satisfied that I had addressed my anxieties of being the 'other' and had raised important contradictions in the Australian Association of Social Work Code of Ethics 2010. My field supervisor was impressed with the review of literature and the depth of the theoretical discussion. However, she noted the 'reflective piece' didn't give her a sense of 'my values/ assumptions/beliefs' that made me notice the particular language people were using in the construction of culturally diverse communities. I remained puzzled about this comment because I thought I had adequately addressed the question of my own 'self'-awareness by addressing my anxieties as a non–white naturalized Australian.

Reflecting back on it now, the process of moving to Darwin and noticing the discernible differences in the social context from Adelaide provided me a sense of comfort and relief that I could channel my anxieties by using reflective learning pedagogy as I progressed and immersed myself with a range of subjects in the social work degree. The comments made by my supervisor continued to bother me and I searched for answers on how to better enmesh my personal histories and my slowly developing recognition of social work as a profession, as I entered a crucial phase of my integration of social work theory and practice.

The final placement: beginnings of a 'critical' turn in my reflective narratives

My final placement was working with individuals, groups and communities in frontline practice in a remote context in Australia. Most of the individuals, groups and communities living in remote communities were from culturally diverse backgrounds. My role as a student on placement in the beginning was to learn, observe, ask questions and take notes. Colleagues and practitioners working in the organization warned me about the 'cultural shock' I would have working and visiting these remote communities. Somehow I never took this seriously because I felt comfortable having lived in India that I was aware of diverse social, cultural and economic environments people lived in.

When I visited these communities the physical environment in terms of the dirt roads and limited infrastructure didn't bother me. However, when visiting and/or interviewing individuals and groups, I started to notice the differences the social and economic infrastructure had on the lives of people. It became apparent that there were few economic opportunities for families and/or adults to work. Whilst many families and individuals were on welfare payments, they usually had one or two community stores with basic necessities, including wheat, sugar, fried takeaway foods, sugary drinks (Coke) and limited fresh fruits/vegetables available. My discussions with community members supported some of the research studies (Altman, 2001; Brimblecombe et al., 2006; Brimblecombe et al., 2013), which noted that accessibility of low cost nutritious food had a significant impact on the community's health. Since we visited these communities during the wet (rainy) season, we couldn't visit some families because roads were closed off and air travel was the only means of contact to urban centers. The remoteness and lack of accessibility by road meant individuals had to travel to cities to avail themselves of many goods and services.

Another major difference that I noticed was the implementation of full and/or partial prohibition in many of the communities (Smith et al., 2013). While I was aware of the policy context in which community leaders in remote communities in the Australian context initiated prohibition, I was troubled by the impact it had on the lived experiences of individuals and communities. For instance, on one of the visits to a remote community, as the plane landed, it is common practice for the police (Clough and Jones, 2004) to search the bags of residents and visitors alike for illicit substances and alcohol. This site at first was very challenging and I thought to myself: imagine your bags being searched to enter your own home! As a practitioner in frontline work, I found it hard to accept that I was subjected to the disciplining technologies of the state (Foucault, 1982) and channeled my anger by arguing that individuals and groups in remote contexts were 'disempowered.' As noted before, during the preliminary visits I was learning about the physical, social and economic context of the environment in which remotely based people in communities lived. Whilst I didn't have the putative cultural shock, what bothered me was the influence, or more precisely how environmental factors influenced, our work with individuals and groups in this context. I read books written by researchers (Mellor, 2002; Trudgen, 2012) who lived and/or worked with culturally diverse communities for four generations. I immersed myself in understanding the social context because I felt as a social worker it is important to locate the context in which one's practice is undertaken. Many of the reflective pieces and meetings with my field supervisor centered on discussing the nuances about the impact colonization had on the social, economic and political milieu of culturally diverse communities in remote contexts. As I worked through gaining a better understanding of the social context, it became clear that my notions of the role of 'social work practice' were embedded in English dominated western practices. It was my field supervisor who drew my attention to the embedded meanings/interpretations of my reflective pieces when she noted: 'Your reflective pieces are conspicuous for the absence of analyzing.

How will you navigate the differences in language and cultural practices?' This observation set me on the path of reflecting on how I approached the question of 'understanding the social context as a social worker.'

As I reflected on my work, it was clear that most of my work had a sociological or, to put a finer point, a structural dimension, not a reflective bent. I felt comfortable jotting down my observations about the social context in which individuals, groups and communities were living. On reflection, it never occurred to me during this phase that I was perpetuating and reproducing anthropological methodologies that firmly centered their 'gaze' on 'understanding people from other cultures.' In my reflective pieces, I didn't unpack why I felt comfortable and didn't have the supposed 'cultural shock' people were warning me about. Neither did I consider the question: Does awareness of diverse social, economic and physical environments equate to lived experiences? I could start to see a pattern, which I have previously referred to in my reflections: my default position is to analyze the sociological and structural aspects of a context, not turn the 'gaze' on the 'self.'

Concurrently, I was mostly observing, learning and taking down notes for the colleagues I was traveling with. In the discussions with my supervisor and the reflective pieces, I started to unpack with certain intensity the language used by colleagues when speaking/interviewing individuals and groups. Having been influenced by the work of Foucault (1982) and Said (1978), I started to become aware of how my own thinking and language had been influenced by my earlier immersion in texts as sites of discursive power. It was personally challenging for me to resist this influential and somewhat comfortable way of thinking and turn my gaze consciously towards my own internal 'talk' and 'text,' and thereby unpack the underlying values and assumptions that influenced my practice as a social worker. As a student I used reflective pieces to channel my observations to reflect more on what underpins social work practice *rather* than unpack how my lived experiences are shaping, influencing and impacting on my developing 'self' as a social work practitioner. I felt reflecting on language and discourse used by other practitioners provided me an opportunity to make a list of the do's and don'ts as a social worker. I took comfort in the thought that at least I can learn by improving my self-awareness of what good practice and bad practice looks like. I also felt comfortable in the thought that as long as I understand the complexities of working with families and children by analyzing the social context and avoid constructing clients in 'deviant language,' I should be fine. However, I continued to resist exploring either in the reflective pieces or with colleagues issues related to what kind of self-awareness I am bringing to my practice and how is it impacting on my frontline work with individuals and groups in a remote context.

My field supervisor was supportive of my reflective pieces but made the observation that I need to start conceptualizing my role as not only an observer and note taker on the field. She suggested that I discuss the possibility of playing a more proactive role in terms of interviewing and/or interacting with clients. This would necessitate that I learn and experience a range of social work skills, including facilitating group interaction, interviewing individuals, families and children. She noted more exposure to frontline work with clients would position me to develop and shape my understanding of the role of a social work practitioner. This suggestion marked the turning point in terms of shaping an awareness of 'self' and my professional identity as a social worker.

This opportunity excited me but I was very nervous about how I will interact with individuals and groups. I had emotions of inadequacy, being unprepared and felt paralyzed because I didn't want to say anything offensive or judgmental. Recognizing my nervousness, my field supervisor suggested we practice skills of interaction with clients through mock scenarios. This process was challenging on various levels: one, my awareness of how language can construct power, two my discomfort and uneasiness of being a social worker who is expected to walk and guide clients on their journeys and, finally, having to apply a predominantly western understanding of 'welfare work' on culturally diverse individuals and groups.

Participating in these practice sessions with my field supervisor laid bare some of the anxieties I had. It emphasized that all the while, I was hiding behind the cloak of feeling comfortable that by using Foucauldian insights on language and disclosure I can critique the structural dimensions of life and not necessarily turn the gaze on myself. This process was confronting because I was aware of the position of power as a social worker, in my interactions with clients. However, this sat in tension with my anxiety of being a 'non-white woman' in a dominant western culture. It was easier for me to address these tensions by identifying myself as the 'other' by positioning myself as a spokesperson speaking on behalf of culturally diverse individuals/groups, instead of working through the position of power that social work conferred on me. These mock practice scenarios and my frontline experience starkly highlighted that all the while I was perpetuating and reproducing the discursive strategies employed by predominant frames of western thinking. I was happy and comfortable to use my gaze to critique these dominant frames but not confront the fact that deep down as a young woman growing up in an educated religious middle class Hindu family in India I had been brought up with paternalistic values. I was encouraged to participate in activities that assisted the socially and economically disadvantaged to broaden my life experience and education.

Also social work in my family was seen as a 'noble' thing to do because it reflected a social conscience. This worldview is very similar to the genesis of social work, which grew out of the need to help the poor, and the downtrodden. All the while, in my reflective pieces I was critiquing the paternalistic attitudes, values and morals that underpin western social work, not recognizing that my own motivation, morals and values were intrinsically tied in the socializing constructs of a middle class approach to social work. Another dimension of my upbringing in India curiously intersected with my anxieties of constructing myself as a non-white, non-English speaking woman in Australia. I asked myself why is it always that my reflective pieces constitute a dominant western 'self' as opposed to non-dominant, non-white other. It occurred to me that growing up in India, it was important to know who the 'other' was. I grew up being socialized into a social context that believed Muslims were physically and culturally inferior because 'they eat meat, they wore gaudy "out there" clothes and didn't wash themselves regularly.' I was discouraged from visiting Muslim friends or classmates and even if I did visit houses of Muslim friends, I was asked to drink tea only. The fact that they eat meat and the knowledge that I would share vegetarian food in those plates was an anathema to maintaining social and cultural purity.

Another significant event that solidified social constructions of discourses of 'good' and 'evil' was the impact two major Hindu serials on Doordarshan (the public broadcaster) had on me as a nine year old. The pictorial brilliance, the dramatic visualization of the discourses of 'good' and 'evil' tied well with broader public debates in the late 1980s and the early 1990s. In the private sphere, watching these serials was a Sunday family ritual. The Sunday routine was organized around the serials and it became an 'event.' It almost seemed these Hindu mythological stories were a way of life and the lessons of cultural differentiation were the way to construct identity.

The embodiment of the dominant self defining the 'other' was evident in my upbringing in India. In my reflective pieces and my discussions during the course of my social work degree, I was using the same heuristic tools that dominant cultures used to define the other. The dominant is obsessed with classifying, categorizing and dividing the body of the other. That is, the narrative clearly says who the other is and what the characteristics are that define them. Ironically, in Australia I started to become aware of how my own thinking had been influenced by the privilege I had grown up with in India. Resisting these influential discourses was difficult, but consciously possible. I realized that I was using the same tools to unpack my own positionality. I was setting up the binary of the 'self' and the 'other' by identifying the characteristics that made me the other and denying the lens of privilege and moral superiority I was countenancing in my developing sense of social work.

Tying together the ambivalent threads of reflective thinking and my developing sense of social work identity

The culmination of working in frontline practice, my moving from Adelaide to Darwin and reflecting on the journey through social work education, was that I realized how my own anxieties have affected my interpretations and understandings of the world. When I began my social work education at an Australian university, I only had a sense that I was uncomfortable and uneasy with the transition from being a Hindu middle class woman to my specificity in a western context. Layered on top of these anxieties were my doctoral studies that had provided me an opportunity to explore in depth how race and nationalism create a dominant self and other.

However, I wasn't sure how all this fitted together at the beginning of my social work education. In the beginning, I felt comfortable that I was being reflective by mentioning that I had a culturally diverse background and my transition from India to Australia was fraught. Most of this reflection was undertaken by fixing my 'gaze' on ways in which dominant discourses operated in social work. Whilst this is an important insight which social work has borrowed from post-structuralist theory, ironically, I discovered through my social work education and my experience in frontline practice in remote communities in Australia that I was following the same heuristic tools used by dominant frames to define the other. This was an important moment in my learning and in the realization of the social work professional self because I am able to acknowledge that my Hindu middle class upbringing in India has had a profound impact on the way I see my practice and the social work profession.

In reflecting on the values, assumptions and beliefs of the social work profession, I was able to turn the 'gaze' on myself and have the confidence to recognize and acknowledge that I need to view my professional social worker self by asking what Walter et al. (2011: 12) argue, 'what are we doing, how are we doing it, what are our assumptions and how are they informed by our privilege.' For me this process of critically laying myself bare is challenging and confronting. It is challenging because I feel I am not part of the dominant white culture and I can feel the difference very keenly, but confronting because despite my feeling like the other, my interpretations and understandings of social work practice were from a position of middle class privilege that I had grown up with in India.

Writing this student narrative has been a very emotional process because the ambivalence I felt towards my transition from an international student to a naturalized Australian has been acknowledged through the opportunity provided by reflective practices embedded within social work education. Whilst the realization of my own privileged position and the way I view and/or interpret the world has ruptured my thinking, I am glad I had the courage to explore and acknowledge the role social work education played in my developing sense of a social worker.

Note

1 As part of the Master of Social Work, students are required to complete two field placements with each of the placements totaling 500 hours.

References

Altman, J. (2001) *Sustainable development options on Aboriginal land: the hybrid economy in the twenty-first century*. No. 226/2001, Centre for Aboriginal Economic Policy, Australian National University.

Australian Bureau of Statistics (2011) *National regional profile: Darwin (Statistical Division)*, Canberra.

Australian Social Work Code of Ethics (2010) Available at www.aasw.asn.au/practitio ner-resources/code-of-ethics

Brimblecombe, J., Ferguson, M., Liberato, S. and O'Dea, K. (2013) 'Characteristics of the community-level diet of Aboriginal people in remote northern Australia,' *Medical Journal of Australia*, 198(7): 380–384.

Brimblecombe, J., Mackerras, D., Clifford, P. and O'Dea, K. (2006) 'Does the store-turnover method still provide a useful guide to food intakes in Aboriginal communities?' *Australian and New Zealand Journal of Public Health*, 30: 444–447.

Carson, D., Ensign, P., Rasmussen, R. and Taylor, A. (2011) 'Perspectives on demography at the edge.' In D. Carson, P. Ramsmussen, P. Ensign, L. Huskey and A. Taylor (eds), *Demography at the edge. Remote human populations in developed nations*, Aldershot: Ashgate, pp. 3–21.

Clough, A.R. and Jones, P.J. (2004) 'Policy approaches to support local community control over the supply and distribution of kava in the Northern Territory (Australia),' *Drug and Alcohol Review*, 23(1): 117–126.

Ennis, G., Finlayson, M. and Speering, G. (2013) 'Expecting a boomtown? Exploring potential housing-related impacts of large scale resource developments,' *Journal of Studies and Research in Human Geography*, 7(1): 33–42.

Ennis, G., Tofa, M. and Finlayson, M. (2014) 'Open for business but at what cost? Housing issues in "boomtown" Darwin,' *Australian Geographer*, 45(4): 447–464.

Foucault, M. (1982) 'The subject and power,' *Critical Inquiry*, 8(4): 777–795.

Mellor, D. (2002) *Many voices: reflections on experiences of Indigenous child separation*, Canberra: National Library Australia.

Said, E. (1978) *Orientalism*, New York: Vintage.

Smith, K., Langton, M., d'Abbs, P., Room, R., Chenhall, R. and Brown, A. (2013) 'Alcohol management plans and related alcohol reforms,' *Indigenous Justice Clearinghouse Brief*, 16.

Taylor, A.J., Carson, D.B. and Ramsey, D. (2014) 'It's raining men in Darwin: gendered effects from the construction of major oil and gas projects,' *Journal of Rural and Community Development*, 9(1): 24–40.

Trudgen, R.I. (2012) *Why warriors lie down and die: towards an understanding of why the Aboriginal people in Arhnem Land face the greatest crisis in health and education since European contact: Djambatj Mala*, Darwin, NT: Aboriginal Resource and Development Services.

Walter, M., Taylor, S. and Habibis, D. (2011) 'How white is social work in Australia,' *Australian Social Work*, 64(1): 6–19.

6

NARRATIVE ABOUT MY JOURNEY THROUGH SOCIAL WORK EDUCATION (FRIDA SVENSSON)

PROFILE

Frida Svensson is a 26-year-old Swedish social work student beginning her seventh and last semester at Gothenburg University. After three years in the program, of which one semester was in India, she is now aiming for further studies at Gothenburg University – the master's program in social work and human rights. Her goal in the future is to work with international social work agencies in so called developing countries.

Introduction

The narrative in this chapter is presented by Frida Svensson from Sweden, as she gives a detailed account of her efforts moving through social work education and fieldwork in India. This international experience was her 'ah-ha! moment' when her habits of being in the world were unsettled, and she writes about her journey through and within this context of change. This narrative also chimes with the earlier narrative, in grappling with 'maps of meaning' in different contexts, bringing personal experiences, organizational and social work cultures and wider social elements to bear in everyday practice. In this reflection space Frida reveals performance of self in specific contexts, raising new questions in attempts to understand self in deeper ways.

★★★

When you're 16, you finish your 'ground education' and have to choose a new school and think about what kind of program you want to study over the coming three years. For me, it was a given that I wanted to study social science. I have always been interested in subjects concerning society and human psychology. Different kinds of injustice have affected me a great deal ever since I was a child. It all starts with childhood and trying to understand why some people don't have the same kind of economical and social safety that I experienced in my life. This thinking developed as I became more interested in society as well as different social and psychological factors that affect a person's life.

After my graduation 2008, I didn't know what I wanted to study. I didn't want to rush into anything; hence I chose to work for a couple of years to gain experience. Many people in my surroundings told me that they thought that social work would be a good fit for me. The social work program here in Gothenburg, Sweden, is very broad and after you graduate, a lot of different opportunities open up, in terms of work and education. I knew that I wanted a job in the future that allowed me to work with people, but also I wanted to contribute to social change.

Without a clear goal or a given path, I began my studies in social work at Gothenburg University. I enjoyed every course, and it literally felt like I was being fed knowledge. In some ways, it felt like putting a puzzle together. All the questions, my curiosity, and sometimes anger, regarding different kinds of social issues in society, became understandable for me. As my education progressed my engagement became deeper and more intense. However, every class concerning our role as professionals within the field felt abstract to me. The practical tools for counseling, documenting or reflection felt further away than the classes about the development of social issues, the big picture and the different kinds of theories. I understood what we were taught, and its significance; still, I had a hard time placing this knowledge in the context of my future role as a professional.

This all changed when I began my fifth semester of fieldwork in India. All of a sudden, classes that had previously felt somewhat abstract, and distant, now became meaningful.

In Sweden, the social work field is extremely broad and I had a difficult time finding where I might best fit in this profession. Through the opportunity to practice in India I was able to reconnect with knowledge I had learnt. I undertook my field internship in Mumbai, India, in a nongovernmental organization. These experiences of practice influenced my understanding of different types of social issues, how the practice of social work is conducted, what kind of theories can be applied, taking into account a new environment and culture. It became clear to me that context determines social issues and practice within the field. I chose the theory of social constructivism to guide my practice in fieldwork. It served as a tool for me so I could be able to gain more understanding of my experiences in the field. For example, I found gender issues present and constructed in a particular way. These social constructions placed values and expectations on women in society. When someone goes against these norms and values, this individual is considered to be problematic and a solution has to be found. In different kinds of societies various categories, values and norms exist and shape the ways social issues emerge. These insights followed me through my practice experience in India and contributed to my thoughts about the importance of reflective thinking in this work.

When I think about my time in India, I often come to think about one special case. I first met the client when the social worker was taking her to the hospital.

The social worker filled me in about all the details of the case and introduced me to a client and her mother. My part in this encounter with the client was to observe and I learned much from this experience. The situation this client found herself in affected me a great deal. She was only 17 years old, unwed and pregnant. The situation of being unwed, a minor and pregnant in India can have devastating consequences and the whole situation was very traumatizing for the girl. I experienced the ways in which values and norms in India created social issues affecting a large part of the population. I constantly had in my mind what this situation would look like in Sweden. What kind of social services would be provided and why? I also thought about how a society looks upon a situation like this and the similarities and differences I could find. In order to do this, I had to reflect upon and understand how and why a situation like this becomes a case that is in need of interventions from social workers.

In class the importance of reflection was emphasized during and after conducting social work practice. On some levels this all made sense to me, but as I mentioned, it became much more abstract when discussing reflection during casework and so on. However, during my time in India, it all fell into place. As mentioned earlier, reflection was something that followed me – both my own reflecting and observing social workers talking about reflection.

I had long discussions with the social worker I observed working with the young woman and her mother. I was curious about how she practiced reflective thinking while working with this family. She told me about four principles that she followed in her work: first it's about acceptance. To accept the client and the current situation she/he may be in. This acceptance has to come with a non-judgmental attitude. For the client to be able to feel safe and comfortable, you as a social worker should keep your own values and opinions aside, and keep a non-judgmental and open attitude. No social worker is totally free from values, opinions, attitudes and feelings regarding different issues in society. Therefore, no one can expect a social worker to be totally neutral when meeting a client. However, it is very important to be aware and reflect about these attitudes, feelings, etc., and how they might affect the client. Through reflection you become aware of your own values, attitudes and feelings even unconsciously present and can avoid them affecting your work with the client. This type of reflection contributes to a professional development that will help you to keep an accepting and non-judgmental attitude.

Self-determination was also one of the principles which remind the social worker that it is always the client's decision. You, as a social worker, are not there to make the decisions for the client. Your role is to support and guide the client. All this will happen with confidentiality. This is something to share with the client, and also give information about the circumstances under which confidentiality might have to be broken.

I could see all these principles come alive in the work of the social worker. Another factor discussed related to when feelings about the family can awaken within you, and the ways to handle these experiences to be able to keep a professional outlook. As discussed above, the case awakened many feelings for me. The social worker paid attention to this, and gave me the time and space to discuss my thoughts and feelings. For me, the meaning of guidance was a dialogue between two different knowledge areas. My supervisor contributes with knowledge, strategies and theories that can help the social worker (and me) to problematize and reflect around the case and client. Good guidance, for me, consists of being supportive and accepting and contributes to personal and professional development. Reflective thinking, in a situation like this, opened up new perspectives. The feelings aroused by my experiences were formed by my perception of reality. So, to be able to understand other people's feelings and reality, I had to understand my own.

To be able to learn from all of my different experiences in India, both as a social work student and as a private person, I needed to be aware of my own understanding of things. First, then, I could open up, learn from and understand what I was experiencing in a country so different to Sweden. Although the social worker assigned to me had little knowledge of Sweden, she understood about my prior experiences and view of social work based upon what I shared with her. Through picturing the situation and the case seen from a perspective that wasn't 'Indian,' but Swedish, she confirmed my feelings and showed me empathy. By showing that she was trying to understand my perspective and way of feeling regarding the client and her circumstances, she also created a place for reflection and mutual acknowledgement. This way of meeting me in this situation also allowed me to gain specific counseling skills, which I will take with me into future practice. She also shared with me her own feelings, experiences and thoughts about different cases and how she was able to have a professional outlook while empathizing with a client's situation. She taught me the importance of taking a step back, and reminding yourself of why you are doing the things you do. She reminded me that you have to think about the context of the organization and your role as a social worker. This, so you can separate what is personal and your profession. To be aware and recognize the feelings and thoughts, you have to be able to reflect about them and use it to develop professionally instead of letting it affect your client.

This process leads us to think about how clients are affected by your reactions and behavior. The social worker stressed the importance of not showing the client if you are emotionally affected. The client may be going through something very emotional and traumatizing and the social worker (and me as a social work student) should operate in a professional way to be able to support the client. Being aware of my presence as it affects relationships, not only the client but also relationships between other professionals, particularly as a foreign student which often attracted attention. This experience raised questions for me while entering, for example, a hospital, hence all the curious looks and questions that appear. This is something that I cannot influence or do anything about. It was a situation that seemed always present during my internship. However, I recognize this, as well as my gender, age, ethnicity and so on, constantly plays a part in not just how people interact with me, but also how I see myself, others, and understand different situations. These experiences were evident in India, as well as in Sweden. Having my practical experience of social work in India might have made this understanding clearer. Sometimes the contrasts became very obvious and things such as my gender or the color of my skin played a huge role in how I was seen or treated. During my education I have been made aware of taking an intersectional perspective in regards to the client and myself.

Another way of discussing how you look at or understand a situation is through theory. During my education there have been a great deal of theories taught and discussed. As I mentioned earlier, strangely enough, these theories never felt abstract to me. We had the opportunity to not just learn the different theories you can use within social work, but also how and why it may be necessary to apply them. They became a tool for me to gain greater understanding regarding social issues and how to work with them. The social worker I worked with provided social services using a systems theoretical approach. When I brought this up with the social worker, she said that she wasn't consciously thinking about a certain theory while working. What I came to think about was what difference would it make if the social worker was aware of what theories she/he had been using. I would say that this brings us back to the discussion regarding reflection. By knowing where the different methods and ways of working are grounded, you become more aware of possibilities. You will also have a greater opportunity to make conscious decisions based on previous knowledge that is comfortable to you and can be effective. As a social work student, I also see it is a way to reflect on your work, practice and hold a critical way of thinking. In my opinion it is a tool to use while conducting social work services and not just as a map for practice. And where it lacks or fails or doesn't match reality, you as a social worker (or student) have to be flexible, critical and use your practical knowledge to develop the theory and decrease the gap between theory and practice.

As I mentioned in the beginning, I had chosen a social constructivist view to describe and understand my experiences in India. You can say that I chose the kind of glasses I was looking through to understand my surroundings and environment. When I chose this lens, I also had to be aware of what this kind of perspective might overlook or miss. The same is true concerning what kind of theories I might use in my fieldwork. It became clear to me how important it felt to be aware of which glasses I was using and why, how this affected what I was seeing and what consequences it could have for possible interventions. A lack of awareness and reflection regarding this, in my opinion, can harm the work that is being conducted – both in the way that the critical thinking can be lost, but also that non-reflected social work and knowledge results in silent knowledge. Silent knowledge doesn't have to be something bad in all situations but after my experience at fieldwork, I witnessed and learned how it sometimes can result in methods failing to develop and move with social change. Work could sometimes be performed without any thought about why you had chosen a particular method. No methods were therefore ever questioned and were constantly in use only because they have always been a stock answer. A lack of reflection and awareness of why you are conducting your work in a certain way affects your professional growth. Without conscious decisions, awareness, reflection and discussions regarding the work, you can prevent professional development. Silent knowledge just stays in one place, while knowledge that is being reflected upon and discussed gets the chance to spread, breathe, evolve and grow.

I understood this experience first hand, when realizing the difference between working with a client where we shared, discussed and reflected together, and working with a client where the only answer to any question would be, 'This is just how we do it.' From working with clients where I had questions but got no answers, or where the work couldn't be explained to me, it was clear that there was no transaction of knowledge gained between any of us. The social workers with this kind of approach also (in my opinion) had a more difficult time connecting with their clients and seemed less interested in their work. For me, this came to set the example of the lack of reflection, self-knowledge and awareness.

However, what I want to underline with all this is how my education is not just something that affects me in conducting practice; it has also strongly influenced me as a person in many ways. My personal growth is constantly shaping my professional growth, and vice versa. These two are intertwined and are constantly contributing to my social work self. I began this narrative speaking about how education was like putting a puzzle together for me. Things fell into place like a puzzle and started to make sense. Upon reflection, before going to India, I knew that social work was the right program for me yet I had a hard time placing myself and could not envision where I would end up in the field. Hence the feeling in some classes that they were too abstract and too specific for me to relate to. My experiences in India changed these feelings and personally these experiences changed me. Professionally, I have finally found what I want to do. It both helped me during my fieldwork experience, but also how I handled the whole experience during a semester in India. This new country with its culture and people enriched me and made me thirst for more. This work also came with many challenges, including ways of seeing, meeting and observing people, contradictions and acceptance. I have experienced attempting to provide social services under circumstances where needs appear to be endless with limited resources. During my time working with this organization I have learned the importance of seeing beyond the wall of contrasts with Sweden. This is their reality, and I and others are there to assist them. There was no alternative but to engage with the social realities in another place, to learn from it and also be a resource for those who struggle or need support. Because exactly as in Sweden, and in every other reality or society, there are people struggling and in need of support. My role as a social worker is to be the support that is needed. In some cases, it's all about the bigger picture, to work with the values and norms that can create extremely difficult situations for different groups in society, and sometimes it's about providing the most basic things and meeting the most basic needs, such as hunger. As a social work student working for the organization in the communities, my role was to start with their social realities, listen to their needs and become a resource for the people so they get the opportunity to make what they can and want with their lives. Thanks to my experience in India – the work, the clients, the social workers, my professor in India and all the amazing people I met there – the last couple of pieces to the puzzle are coming together and I am now aiming for a future within international social work.

7

UNENDING EXPEDITION

A reflective account of my journey to the social work profession (Yogita Naruka)

Introduction

In the beginning paragraphs of this narrative, Yogita tells of her experiences in education as the springboard to her journey through social work education. She describes the development of the profession in India mostly in response to industrialization and ongoing inequalities in society. The narrative gives a detailed account of social conditions in her fieldwork practice and integrating this work with theory on the practice floor. The story she tells reflects the realities of practice in difficult and often extreme social conditions and learning through social work education. She has a sense of being in the 'thick of it' – as social conditions are tied to structural issues, social development and inequalities. This practice story describes self-perspectives along the way to close the gap between reflective practice and working for and through social change.

***

I would have never been able to make sense of calling of my life if I had not entered the academic world of social sciences in a way that I could. Being a student of science at the higher secondary level, I always faced a disjunction between my convictions and what my education was trying to deliver to me. Though I learnt and scored well by learning the formulae of chemistry and principles of physics, these formulae and principles never answered the questions related to identity, sexuality, gender, etc. growing inside a teenager's mind. This bewildered mind gained refuge in a random decision of pursuing graduation in Elementary Education. This proved to be a gateway to academics of social sciences, an opportunity to discuss and share my life experiences with my peers and faculty. The coursework and training for four undergraduate years was an interesting journey through the concepts of education, learning, cognition, self and identity by constant association of these with lived experiences. It not just addressed the questions with which I was grappling to a certain extent but it also gave a direction for the future course of my academic life. The decision to pursue a higher academic journey into a sociology related discipline emerged from here and resulted in the selection of social work as my discipline post-graduation.

The transition from graduation to post-graduation was rather smooth for me compared to those of my friends who entered social work after their graduation in non-social science disciplines. The initial struggle to locate myself in sociological discourses was already over for me. Rather, I was looking forward to an interesting and enriching journey that could provide me with learning about new issues, provide me with knowledge to develop strong perspectives and get necessary skills to apply my knowledge in the practical world. With such expectations I began my social work education and that initiated a new course in my life. Of late, social work as a professional degree course has received much attention from students and the development sector in India. Unintended outcomes of development, economic reforms, rapid urbanization, industrialization and changing labor market dynamics have given rise to glaring inequalities in the social fabric. This unequal social fabric has also raised the issues of some disenfranchised identities who have been continually neglected in the mainstream of development. All this has called for an organized practice to bring forth the issues and voices of disempowered communities and individuals and work with them in a systematic way. While other social science disciplines like sociology and political science have been theorizing the phenomena related to such unequal societies and have helped students understand the causality behind these phenomena, social work practice aimed at bringing out solutions to the crisis that societies have been facing. Social work thus has emerged as the bridge between theory and practice and is aimed at developing professional social workers with skills to work with individuals, families and communities. This practical aspect of the social work program was most enticing to me when I decided to pursue it as a career.

Theory and practice is linked in the social work program through immediate exposure of students to the fieldwork and continuing the same throughout the duration of the degree program. As part of the master's program in social work, our department too had mandatory concurrent fieldwork for students. Students were placed in fieldwork settings, which were either non-profit organizations, schools, hospitals, shelter homes, etc., or open community settings. Working with communities and marginalized groups in urban as well as rural areas and engaging with problems arising out of poverty, inequalities and breakdown of social relations and community life were the initial thrust areas of social work practice in India. The tradition still holds much value and communities in urban areas like slum communities are vital social work practice territories.

Our department has been following this tradition and students work with locals of slum and resettlement communities in Delhi every year as part of their social work fieldwork practicum. I also went to one of the slum communities situated on the eastern bank of Yamuna River in Delhi for fieldwork with four others. This was a firsthand exposure to the problems and issues about which we kept talking about in classrooms. This became a platform where we could apply the classroom knowledge and learn by experience. At the same time, it was equally challenging as we had to carve our path on our own and we had minimal support from any organization working there. Continuous guidance from the supervisor from our department helped us gain some very basic skills to work in such a community where one does not have any specific scope of work defined for oneself. Elementary skills like interacting with people, forming a rapport with them, identifying needs and issues of the community, locating resources and areas of concern for communities, establishing tie-ups with the organizations and people of relevance in such places became some of my key learning which kept on improving with time.

The terrain of fieldwork in social work practice poses challenges for everyone. Every practitioner, I believe, gets to face the challenges specific to their field. In the community field setting one of the major challenges is to keep your 'self' dissociated from the lives of people in the community and maintain a balance as someone to whom people can look for support and information and as a facilitator who is there just to guide people. Community settings always put a practitioner under a pile of expectations from the people for getting their work done. I faced similar situations in my field settings where people expected me to do work for them. Mere facilitation was inadequate and insufficient for them. Maintaining the role of a facilitator and helping people to develop their capacities to help themselves through providing information and enabling them to access institutions was one part of dissociation of self from people for me.

The second aspect of dissociation of self is more at an emotional level. I was often faced with instances when I encountered stories of extreme poverty, exploitation, violence, sexual assaults either as incidents or as moving narrative accounts from people. Such situations left me many times shaken, moved and perplexed on my role as a listener of such narratives. The calm approach that I learnt to take over time by keeping an emotional restraint on myself is a very subtle virtue that I developed through fieldwork practice. Fieldwork practice helped me in dealing with these situations in a professional way and take up suitable action for them. These virtues and skills hold much importance in my journey of social work practice as they could be learnt only through the direct fieldwork experience. Theories and books did teach me values, ethics and skills of social work but mere textual reading was always a bland and dissociative exercise. Concurrent field experience helped me to relate to such textual exercises more and relate to them in a better way.

Along with skills, virtues and values, a specific contribution of working in a slum community has been on developing the nuanced understanding of various issues that most of the communities have been facing in India, like community health concerns, supply side issues in public distribution systems, ineffective educational institutions, inconsistencies in dissemination of incentives and benefits of various government schemes to people, and the impact of such problems on the life of people. Interaction with people, doing needs assessment with them, conducting participatory research appraisal activities with them helped me strengthen my knowledge on some significant issues related to social development in the country. No doubt that this was also because of the classroom lectures, but field experience layered the theoretical information with practical and ground level realities.

Apart from the community setting, I also had the opportunity to work with an organization working with people suffering from drug abuse, for their recovery and rehabilitation. Unlike the community setting, my interactions here were more structured, conscious and deliberate. Though the area of work of the organization was not much related to my area of interest, it became a unique experience in itself to be a part of a community which has little interaction with the outside world and understand the nuisances of recovery from the perspective of people who were going through it. Spending more and more time in this structured setting and in-depth interactions with patients, their families, staff and counselors gradually helped me develop the perspective with which every stakeholder was looking at the process of recovery. This combined with reading about the models of recovery for drug addiction helped me develop my critical understanding about the treatment process, which I tried sharing with the organization too. Casework and counseling were significant learning for me during this period. This was also a crucial experience in learning about the organizational setup, their mandate to work according to vision and objectives, administrative procedures and critical issues that an organizational set up in the development sector can face.

Though fieldwork practicum helped students develop some skills, which could not be learnt through classroom teaching, still there was a helplessness that I always felt during the course of fieldwork. This helplessness was related to the location of the cause of problems with which I was dealing during my fieldwork. I was working with the communities, which were grappling with the issues of drug abuse, poverty, unemployment, weak governance systems, gender discrimination and marginalization of minorities. Theoretical understanding helped me understand these problems as part of larger structural systemic failures rather than as standalone issues. Reflecting on my fieldwork, I found the fieldwork practice to be just providing the temporary solutions to problems rather than addressing the cause of the problem itself. Addressing the main cause of problems, which is often associated with the nature of government policies and actions and their improper implementation, seemed to be out of reach as a student social work practitioner. Also, as a discipline, social work practice aims to develop professional social work practitioners who would in future try to influence the systems and structures with the knowledge and skills acquired during their academic training. These confusions and face offs with structural problems and locating one's own role in such a situation were then in a way a necessary exercise. These set a preparatory ground for the future professional journey where one can actually utilize one's capacities to interact with the system and attempt to address the main cause of the problems. But as a student social worker, the only solace was in enabling people to ask for their rightful claims as citizens within the unaccountable and weak governance systems.

Fieldwork stands as a link between theory and practice. Therefore, fieldwork in social work practice, I believe, does not end in the field itself. Rather it is followed up by the activities of expression and classroom discussions. This follow up is extremely important as it enables students to make sense of their field experiences, critically assess their actions in the field and outcomes of those actions, learn from others' experiences and do a ground assessment of the theories that they usually study in the classroom. Moreover, I always felt that there is a very strong impact of such activities on the overall temperament of students as the platforms of shared and cooperative learning provide students with the qualities of being a good listener, improve their communication and expression, hone their presentation skills and help them become more patient in working with sensitive issues. This in turn has a huge role in developing students as professional social workers for the outside practical world.

As an individual I must acknowledge that I did learn the basics of writing academic papers, which are quite useful to me at present in my research degree course. Also, by being critical in certain ways about the functioning of these conferences and by reflecting on the scope of improvement, I did develop and learn my own ways to participate and conduct conferences in professional life. Though skills at this level kept on improving with increasing experience, the fundamental skillset was developed at the stage of social work education only. This indeed has an important contribution towards my headway as a development professional. Like group conferences, individual conferences were also made a compulsory part of the curriculum in which students were expected to discuss their fieldwork activities with their supervisors (supervisors were faculty members allocated by the department to each student at the time of fieldwork placement). Individual conferences provided a more relaxed setting to students to discuss their various concerns and plans related to fieldwork. An important contribution of these meetings was that these provided an opportunity to discuss some of the conflicts and dilemmas related to fieldwork which students usually could not discuss during group conferences. During my fieldwork, I could get optimum use of these meetings for which the major reason was the time that my faculty supervisors devoted to listen to my concerns. These meetings many times gave me clarity in planning my actions and activities in the field setting. However, as a general trend within the department, it was quite evident that utility of such meetings depended directly upon the time that faculty supervisors could give to students on a regular basis. In the absence of such devotion on the part of both faculty and student, these meetings remained of no use.

Another major follow up of fieldwork was the task of report writing which was expected to be reflexive as well as connecting field experiences to theoretical knowledge. Not just a mandatory requirement for completing the degree but regular fieldwork reports were expected to be reflexive, theoretically rich and should have a glimpse of what goes through one's mind while working in the field. Now, I must admit that reflexive writing is a skill that one develops over a period of time and one would need a devotion of specific time and energy for this. This kind of writing gets improved after each piece, provided one gets the right kind of feedback and suggestions. Speaking solely from my own experience, gradually these reports in social work program are treated as just a record of events and become a mundane exercise lacking the essence of reflection. I certainly believe that in order to make the whole process interesting and enriching for students, well concentrated efforts towards helping students develop the art of writing as well as discussing these reports are required.

Fieldwork being a very crucial element takes much importance within the social work curriculum. But classroom teaching has its own place. At the onset of discussing about the classroom teaching, I must share that social work has a quite balanced curriculum with a fine balance of pure sociological theories, critical issues of development, different approaches to professional social work, and research skills and techniques. The journey might have had gaps but indeed it has helped me grow professionally. Wide areas of choices available as an intern with different organizations and flexibility in choosing the placements has helped me to experiment with my skills and get a variety of experience. Ranging from pure ground level activism to a structured organizational set up, two years of the journey of social work provided enriching experiences. Internships provided vibrant experience of being a professional in the world of practice. It enabled me to break boundaries and move out of the comfort zone, widened the capability set, understand the realities of the world of practice, which were many times conflicting to what I studied. Closely working with different organizations working on the ground by being part of their structure helped not just to understand the conflicts between the world of theory and world of practice but it also provided avenues and spaces to reconcile these conflicts. This happened many times through feedback, appraisals, interactions with organization leaders and colleagues, reflective writing and sometimes plainly through thinking within myself and amicably solving the dilemmas within me.

Today, when I reflect back while writing this, I must admit that two years of social work education was indeed a significant platform of my life. It has not just given a specific direction to my professional career but it has helped me realize what I was expecting from my profession and enabled me to get close to that. I would also confess that the whole journey, beginning from making a shift from science to social science and later taking up social work as a career option has not been very smooth at a personal level. It has been full of struggles (some of them are still on) and largely these struggles have a lot to do with my identity of being a woman from an Indian middle class family. Deciding on social work as an option of education and career raised doubts in the minds of many for being an unconventional career option and not being financially lucrative enough. Many people who still understand social work as the work of charity have expressed to me their doubts over social work as a professional career option. Tender years of career building often tend to put one in doubt about one's own decision due to such remarks from people around. Moreover, working with the marginalized communities and groups and traveling to remote locations instead of sitting in luxurious offices is still less encouraging career territory for females in India. All this has led to a major struggle for me to put across my career choice with confidence and a choice as valid as any other conventional job. Consistent debates and arguments about taking up social work as a career choice have often put me into spells of irritation and frustration. These feelings grew stronger when I had to explain the significance and importance of the work I do or intend to do when I believe that work that is being taken up by this profession is certainly the need of the hour.

Nevertheless, over the period of time, the struggles, debates and arguments with others have strengthened my conviction in my choice. It has made me stand more strongly towards my values and ideals in life. Being fully aware that my work can make a difference to lives of a few people not merely gives immense satisfaction but also makes me more convinced in the choices and decisions that I have made. I must admit that over all these years and until the present moment I am evolving as a mature and sensitive human being and I owe this largely to the varied experiences that I have been exposed to during years of educational training as well as while working with different development organizations. I strongly believe that the profession, which involves an explicit agenda of change, would remain unfulfilled if professionals involved in it lacked commitment to it and did not possess sensitivity to issues of people they work with. Also, the commitment and vision of change is halfhearted if one remains dissociated from it in one's personal life. Over the years of education and practice I have realized that in a development profession, there is no separation of personal and professional; rather it is personal values that drive one to take up such a trajectory in life and strive for it. Many times, I have experienced moments of conflicts and dilemmas regarding the larger utility and purpose of certain actions, clash with personal values, but patience and diligence developed over the period of time due to educational and professional experience have enabled me to find possibilities of resolving these conflicts without compromising on personal ethics and values. Continuous reflection on my actions and decisions has indeed been one strong approach for resolving these conflicts. I hope to continue to work for the values that I stand for in future and keep learning from and reflecting on my experiences.

8

REFLECTIVE NARRATIVE (LAYLA SEWELL)

Introduction

In this narrative, Layla begins with an open discussion about reflection through self and broader social contexts. These intersections are explored in detail shifting through personal experiences in childhood and in social work education. In the telling of her story, empowering words from family, ancestors and cultural icons drive self-perspectives.

★★★

Before writing this narrative, I cruised through life without true self-reflection. The social work program at California State University, Dominguez Hills emphasizes self-reflection; however, I was more consumed with a critical race theory paradigm. Each semester, the students in the program must complete eight process recordings that include multiple questions about self-reflection. In addition, the practicum class requires one to two assignments on either our personal narrative or about self-reflection. As a student, I took this for granted and treated the assignments as an unnecessary task, and thought about just doing the bare minimum. After receiving feedback on the first draft of this narrative, I realized I have been a shallow person when it comes to looking at who I am, what I represent, and what I stand for. In the field, I can discuss others' pathology and strengths or explain a client's motivation; however, I have a challenge differentiating my own values and assumptions.

My life experiences, my environment, and my thought process make me a human being. I embraced all of my social identities, which include being an African American woman who is married with two children, but I am much more than that. By knowing more about my own motivations, drives, and biases allows me to demonstrate cultural humility and competence in the social work field. Although I have been to therapy in the past and have had supervision with my field instructor, it was not until recently that I started thinking about my inner working model. During counseling and supervision, I skated by with discussing external issues. Not until my last therapy session and a current discussion of one of my process recordings, did I find out how detached I am from looking at how and what my thought processes are. My therapist asked me multiple times how I feel about a situation and if I shared my feelings with my husband. Each time, I would struggle to look inside to process where my feelings and thoughts are coming from. The same thing happened when a supervisor asked me how did I use my professional self when I was conflicted about a family ordered to do numerous classes such as domestic violence, parenting, anger management and counseling at the same time while trying to raise their teenagers. She was able to help me look at myself before judging the family predicament. What do I draw from myself that can provide the best practice for this family? I was baffled at how I was unable to answer that question immediately. While it bothered me that I am not in touch with myself, it was easy to let it go because it takes peeling some deep seeded layers to get to the stuff I easily avoided for these 38 years.

Perhaps being raised by my divorced parents affected my pathological detachment. My parents were young and my father was in the military. I was fortunate to have two loving parents, but the constant changing of locales affected my ability to develop a strong sense of self. Every one to two years, I had to meet new friends and get accustomed to learning new social norms. There were years when I was an extrovert and there were years when I was an introvert. There were years where I would be living with my father on a prominently white Air Force base, followed by a move to live with my mom in a black, low-income area and was chastised for talking and dancing white. Or when residing in Montana, my brother and I were the only black students in the entire school. Consequently, I was a target of hate crimes and racial discrimination. At times, my choices were limited to avoid confrontation and violence. There were times when I was compelled to defend my younger brother and myself by fighting ourselves out; either defend myself or become a victim. Unfortunately, there was not anyone to process this for me. I look back now on how important it is to be able to process any transition in my life.

Now I am able to look back on how some experiences have shaped the essence of Layla. When I was younger, living with my mother, I recall one of the first times where I felt less than and cared about what others thought about me. My mother was a working single mother and the after school day care providers used to snicker about how unfortunate we are to have a single mother and how we will probably end up down the wrong path. We went to school on base, so most of the families were two-parent households at that time. I felt isolated and ostracized because my parents did not live together like the other kids. In retaliation, I stole another child's cassette tape, which perpetuated what they thought of me. A year or two later when I was in the fifth grade, I remember going to a mega church with my white friend's family. I attended a few times because I enjoyed the sense of belonging. At that time, I was with my father and we lived on base with no extended family in the near vicinity. One day during communion, the priest put his hand on my shoulder and looked at me with a crooked smile and said non-chalantly, 'I'm glad you come to our church even though you are the only black person here.' I was mortified. I turned around and realized that I was the only black person. I then started internalizing that everyone must think about me being the only black person there. I suddenly felt like I did not belong and felt unwel-comed. I never went back and never told my friend why. Once again I did not have the opportunity to process what I felt and what was actually reality.

Even as an adult working in the male dominated film industry, I never quite felt like I deserved to be in leadership positions. I was young at the time, producing films, and I was in charge of crews of 20–60 people. On one particular film shoot, a cinematographer who was old enough to be my father did not like the fact that he had to answer to me. There was a time that I had to confront him about overstepping his boundaries with another crewmember. He blew up on me, chastising me that I do not know what I am doing and that he's worked in this business long before I was even born. I held my ground on the outside, but internally I ques-tioned myself. Instead of inside conversations such as 'how can I gain respect from him so he can see that I am competent and worthy of this position,' I instead started asking myself self-defeating questions. Do I belong in this position? Can I handle this level of work? I kept these insecure thoughts to myself because sharing them with another would show weakness and inferiority.

Although I had insecurities, I always went for what I desired. I pursued my goals with underling insecurities and self-doubt. I still accomplished great things in my life like running a film festival, held executive positions and started non-profit organizations. Luckily, my drive to have a positive impact on people's lives over-powered my thoughts of inadequacy. Caring about what others thought of me has stayed with me from a child moving from city to city and is still a challenge I deal with to this day. Perhaps my passion to awaken the greatness in others stems from my own feelings of incompleteness. I have always had a burning desire to empower or motivate others to better themselves and have a better life. Perhaps I get joy out of helping others to one day get to the point where I operate from my best self. To get to that point, self-reflection opens a path for discovery of the intricate workings of Layla.

Coming into the Master of Social Work program at the ripe age of 38 scared the living daylights out of me. When I walked into class, I felt the same feelings of starting a new school when I was younger switching schools every year. My automatic thoughts included: Will I connect with anyone? Everyone is so young.

Am I smart enough to do the work after so many years since college? Once I realized that the topics were relevant to my previous work and volunteer experience, I knew I was in the right place. It was far from easy. I am a type of person that will blab my business but who is tight with her feelings. The papers I had to write certainly challenged me to open up and dig deep to uncover my inner motivations, thoughts, and feelings. I had to step out of my comfort zone to critically analyze theoretical applications and practice as well as current trends. Writing my two cents did not cut it like it did in the past. I second guessed my public school and undergraduate education for preparing me for this kind of writing. My insecurities from childhood resurfaced.

In this program, I have found myself pulled in different directions because I want to challenge, fix or change the deficits in the social work field in different areas and all at one time. The great thing about the social work profession is that there are vast opportunities to pursue; yet on the other hand, it may be hard to choose a direction. My first year in the Master of Social Work program, I was placed in a department that served girls who were victims of commercial sexual exploitation of children, so I became engrossed in that arena. Then I began interest in the lack of action the child welfare institutions took on the disproportionality and disparity of families of color in the system and then I found interest in foster care advocacy. If it were not for the big picture that I have for my non-profit organization, Awaken the Greatness Foundation, I would be all over the place and scattered about which path to choose.

Being a student in the social work program has opened my understanding in reflecting on how intersectionality can be useful to understand individuals. Although people are socially constructed to be labeled in certain social economic statuses or ethnic groups, within these groups, people have different values and their own diverse thought processes. It has helped me to become aware of why I have always felt like I never truly fit in one box and felt contradictory feelings of inadequacy and empowerment at the same time. People carry multiple identities and have overlapping interests where injustices may intersect. Taking advantage of self-reflection as a student gives me an opportunity to grasp how social construction may place different ethnicities into specific classifications. This allows space to take a critical stance toward shared assumptions. My thoughts and perceptions of myself affect how I react to others, and understanding my own narrative will help me differentiate my underlining biases of others.

Critical race studies has created a lens to help me understand how racism is constructed and why it still exists. It gives me deeper understanding on why it will take many more generations for African Americans to be on equal footing with majorities when it comes to self-worth and access. We can only go so far with confidence and self-worth, but because of systemic oppression, being the wrong color at the wrong place and wrong time can be a fatal situation. White Americans do not share the same cautionary tale with their entitled privilege. The systems set forth have created disenfranchised communities with a poor quality of life with a lack of physical, mental, and social freedom.

As a social worker, it is my duty to advocate for others; I must consider the social construction that has created the barriers and struggles that my clients face. Applying critical race theory to my practice calls for continued personal reflection and self-correction, hence, I will not fail my clients due to my lack of understanding of privilege, personal bias, etc. I must continue personal growth and development to where I continuously analyze models of assessment, prevention, intervention and evaluation by continuing to produce and implement programming through my organization and proceed with effective and culturally relevant practice while I'm in the field of social work. I must take advantage of opportunities to bring the critical race theory perspective to people who may not realize that their privilege or bias could affect their ability to effectively advocate for their clients.

Working with victims of child sex trafficking in my first year of the master's program, I found myself frustrated that these young women were flaky and did not have common sense to follow up on their business. Through continuous education I learned how trauma affects people in different ways and that most people are not developmentally able to be handed a referral and follow up to take care of their business. Although some of these young ladies were over 18, pieces of their childhood and life skills education were missing. Looking at a person in their environment sets the stage as to why we are needed to help them navigate this 'normal' world when they have experienced a chaotic one. I continually work at humbling myself when working with others. I am aware that I love to give advice on everything. I am cognizant that it is better to talk less and listen more. When I am present and genuine, I get the best outcomes. When I listen intently, I am better able to assess a situation. This awareness influences me to be a better observer in practice by letting the situation reveal itself instead of making assumptions.

Self-reflection is key to being effective in helping marginalized and oppressed populations. As an African American woman, I have faced many challenges; however, I am cognizant of the privileges that I hold. I grew up with parents who loved and supported me. I am privileged that I am happily married with two children and have no financial burdens. I have transportation and multiple options to choose where to live and where to send my children for their education. Because I am heterosexual, I will never have to experience the challenge of coming out of the closet or making sure my sexuality does not make others feel uncomfortable. As an American, I may be part of the dominant ideology as opposed to immigrants; nonetheless, I do not feel a part of the dominant culture. I do not have the power, privilege or influence as someone who would be considered part of the dominant culture. I have been educated by dominant ideologies through public school and the media; however, I had an environment supportive enough to allow me to challenge the norm and seek truth for myself. This truth of cultural pride built upon my already inert resiliency that stemmed from childhood. My intersectional identities add dimension and counter-storytelling to the status quo. While this can be an asset to the social work profession when working with diverse groups, it is a life long process to be culturally competent and to practice cultural humility. I aim to not separate myself from others, thinking I am beyond flaws or that I am superior. I accept that my clients and I will have a reciprocal relationship as, through them, I will learn more about myself and the world, as much as they may learn from me. We all have experiences that other people can learn from, whether it is for new ideas, understanding or compassion. That is how I am able to utilize 'use of self.' Use of self is adapting to the individual and not succumbing to the stereotypical construct that surrounds them. I work on checking my biases at the door so I may be open to validate and affirm another individual's perspective. We all have a narrative and sometimes people just want to be understood. I am reminded of this when I am cursed out by clients who are frustrated because they feel trapped in a world that does not understand them and cannot envision a way to get out of their situation without pain and suffering.

When I was in the multilevel marketing industry, I had the opportunity to take advantage of personal development. Every time I heard someone speak or partici-pated in some empowerment exercise, I wanted to take the same information and experience to marginalized populations. I felt if they received the same messages as I did, they would be better off. I thought of Maya Angelou's famous quote: 'When you know better, you do better.' Now that I look back, I was acting as if I was an authority figure of what is best for others without considering their perspective. My social work education has influenced me to be open to other people's pro-cessing and how they react to their environment. How I would do things is not necessarily the best for others.

I am a believer of Sankofa, meaning to look back, as I pull upon my ancestors for strength and resilience. I am a descendent of the Africans who survived the Ma'afa, also known as the transatlantic slave trade. I am a descendent of the African Americans who survived lynching and Jim Crow. I am a direct descendent of my father, Wilbur Sewell, who served in the military, built his house with his own hands, went back to school to get a bachelor's degree and now helps take care of his mother who has Alzheimer's. I am a direct descendent of my mother, Debbie Patton, who was discarded by the community as a troublemaker as a teen mother, but defied odds with a flourishing career in the department of corrections and raised two lovable children. She is now the one to go to for money, advice and to look over her intellectually disabled niece.

The person I bring to the social work practice is the person who is influenced by Oprah Winfrey, with big ideas on how to change the world as well as influenced by Cuzin Sista, my great grandmother, who impacted her neighborhood by being a model of unconditional love for others in the community. I bring a person who is a work in progress when it comes to unyielding confidence and will help others not allow negative circumstances to limit their aspirations. I bring an awareness to consider all sides of the story and an understanding of the context. I bring a person who aims to operate at the highest vibration.

9

MY JOURNEY THROUGH SOCIAL WORK EDUCATION (NICOLE JONES)

PROFILE

Nicole Jones is a graduate student in the Master of Social Work program at California State University, Dominguez Hills. She received her bachelor's degree from California State University, Monterey Bay, where she studied Communications. Nicole has written for the Los Angeles Sentinel *newspaper and worked in radio in Los Angeles. Currently she is interning as a school social worker for the Los Angeles Unified School District. She is passionate about education and is a lifelong learner. In the near future, she anticipates doing research and earning her doctoral degree. She loves spending time with her family, traveling, and reading novels.*

Introduction

In the narrative in this chapter, Nicole opens by looking at her motivations for a career in social work. Her narrative tells us about her experiences of racism in its many forms, including wider cultural narratives and focus on structural inequalities. She relates her introduction to reflection in social work and the opportunity it provides to examine her story in different ways.

★★★

The field of social work was not my first career choice. I come from a journalism/public relations background filled with celebrity interviews, red carpet events, award shows and after parties. I wanted to be the next Oprah Winfrey. Coming from such a glamorous field, one would ponder why I am pursuing social work. I knew nothing about social work, nor what practice entailed. However, being in this program I have come to realize that social work is so much more than handling cases, diagnosing, and assessing individuals. Social work is a practice that truly puts a mirror up to one's face and shows them who they really are. All the altered perceptions, biases, prejudices, and unexamined issues in one's own life slowly start to show through an individual's exterior and all of these things start to help put everything one thought about life into perspective, and helps them come to the realization that they – at the core of their existence – have things they need to address in order for them to truly understand who they are, where they are going, and the person they want to become moving forward.

In the short amount of time I have been in this program, studying social work theory and practice has done this for me. Coming into this program I did not know what to expect, and now I have embarked on a whole new world and a whole new way of thinking that makes me question everything about my life as it relates to who I am as a black woman in a world that is entrenched in systems of oppression that keep minorities in the continuous cycle of injustice. I grew up in the heart of Los Angeles, and unlike the majority of African American children I know, with both of my parents and younger brother. One would describe my neighborhood as the 'hood,' where homelessness, gang activity, and prostitution are a way of life. However, though in these surrounding conditions, my parents, who were full time workers, managed to keep my brother and I sheltered from the chaos. Growing up, I never felt poor or marginalized, I had everything I needed and oftentimes more, and I was always able to participate in my school activities. As a young girl, my parents taught me to never see color and because where I lived, went to school, and church, everyone looked like me, I had no reason to feel inferior about who I was. I had never experienced racism from another race. In fact, it was my auntie who first helped me realized that I was an 'other.'

When I was five years old I loved baby dolls, I loved everything about playing dress up with them and combing their silky satin like hair. It was not until my auntie asked me, 'Nicole, why don't you have any baby dolls that look like you?' that made me wonder why was this the case, and what did a baby doll that looked like me look like? The skin tone of the white baby dolls that I owned never bothered me, my parents just wanted to make me happy and get me the dolls I desired. The fact that there were not many dolls that were designed with dark skin tones was not an issue for my parents. When my auntie bought it to my attention and my parents' attention, my parents still were very nonchalant about it because I do not think revelations like that affected them. I do not believe they cared if I had a collection of dolls of every skin tone, this was something they were not conscious about. However, every time I went to the toy store thereafter, I made sure that my parents knew that I wanted a doll that looked like me. I did not get the doll that looked like me right away, but when I did her name was Kenya. I remember her design very vividly. She was very dramatic, she was from Kenya, she wore tribal print clothing, her hair was a lot rougher than my other dolls, and she still was not my chocolate complexion, she was more of a peanut butter shade, but I was still happy that I had finally had a black baby doll and I asked my auntie did she look like me and she said 'close enough.' Unbeknownst to me then, I began to learn about the social construction of race. Although I did not fully understand my auntie's intentions, at that young age I unconsciously started to think critically about what message was being sent down the toy aisle after my auntie's observation. The lack of diversity in toys is a subtle way of society dismissing what they feel is inferior. This example of micro-aggressions is constant in everyday conversation, and studying social work has made me more aware of these subtle instances that are more overtly offensive than one makes them out to be. I think of this experience as a precursor to what I would experience throughout my life not only as an African American woman but as a darker skinned African American citizen. Micro-aggressions, subtle segregation, prejudice, and colorism are still prevalent, not only from other backgrounds, but they lie within my own culture as well.

Later, as I grew up, I started to see patterns of these issues thread in and out of my life. I reflect that how my parents informally taught me not to see color has enabled me to be naive about the world and how society views me or how I am supposed to be. As a black woman in society I am not supposed to be educated, articulate, cultured. I am not supposed to travel outside of the country, or have the resources I need to be great in every aspect of my life, but I have done all these things and I do have the resources to be great. Growing up and even now I do not assume others are putting me in a box because of me being a black woman, but what I have learned is that they do. Going to a university that was only 4 percent African American, I experienced the sense of being an 'other' after specific events dealing with racial slurs being spelled out across the main quad or casually walking across campus to class, while people yelled out derogatory names to my friends and I. These were memorable experiences that allowed me to see that in some ways and to some people neither I, nor my peers who looked like me, were accepted. This act of negligence and ignorance inspired me as the vice president of Black Students United (BSU) to always make it a priority to be present on campus through events, seminars, protests, etc. I believe that some people thought that writing slurs and name calling was not a big deal, because the media glamorizes social issues to the extent they are no longer issues and at some point they get ignored. I always knew that I wanted to go to college, and my environment and where I grew up never swayed my decisions on pursuing higher education. I never thought that getting into college was hard. I was always a hard worker and over achiever so I knew that I had what it took to get there, I just did not know how I would. There were several mentors in my life to help me navigate through the application process, along with the help of my parents giving me the support and confidence that I needed. I wanted to do something more with my life. My parents gave me and my brother a great and exciting life, and I always thought that there could be more adventure. I found my excitement in reading books and I loved going to school. I was blessed to have amazing teachers who have become lifelong mentors and inspirations in my life. Their encouragement and insight is what has inspired me to pursue beyond a master's degree. I was immensely influenced by their work ethic and knowledge that I wanted to be to others what they were to me.

This motivation to help and inspire others is what influenced my pursuit in the social work program. I am not so much concerned with the micro practice of social work but the macro, simply because macro focused social work transcends and does not just focus on self, however the ironic thing about wanting to pursue macro practice is I must know how the micro affects the macro. Simply put, I must know myself before I can know and serve others on a greater level.

This idea of reflection is so provocative and such an excellent skill to acquire in the social work profession and in life. As I reflect on the training I am getting currently in my field placement as a school social worker, I am reminded of the population that I serve – elementary school students. I think about how I was at their age, and how everything was true and became my reality. Wiser now, I know this to be so far from the truth and this makes me explore myself even more. Looking at the students I often think about what I would have wanted someone to tell me at their age that would have lessened the sting of someone teasing me or the importance of being in that moment because I will never get it back again. I think about how I am learning the importance of knowing my own issues and how self is deeply explored throughout the curriculum. Learning about the ways to conduct sessions and being aware of one's effect and learning about how being culturally competent in the profession is helping me recognize how unaware I am of my own cultural bias and prejudices.

This program's main focus is on the micro and I do understand why, reflecting on oneself and realizing how they can or cannot serve the client is crucial. Knowing oneself and recognizing bias populations is a wise revelation for a prac- ticing social worker to have, and one can only do this by being self-aware and reflecting on the why within themselves.

I started writing in a journal when I was in the sixth grade and I have not stopped. Being consistent with these journal entries, I believe that my writing has helped me figure out a lot of 'whys' and obstacles in my life. Writing and reflecting has always allowed me to recognize the root of whatever situation I was going through. As I think about who I was in the sixth grade and who I am now, there is immense change, not only physically, but mentally, spiritually, and intellectually. Recently, I have read through some of my journal entries from high school and middle school. Although I have lived what I have written, reading through the years has allowed me to see how reflecting on one's life brings a vulnerability.

Vulnerability, or being vulnerable is something people usually shy away from because it implies that one may be weak, soft, hyper sensitive, and the list goes on. On the contrary, to be vulnerable is to be strong, enlightened, determined, and possibly motivated to change what may be making one unguarded. To be vulnerable is to know oneself well enough to understand that perfection is impossible. No one is perfect. We all have insecurities, flaws, and shortcomings. All these imperfections are what make us unique. My engagement with the reflective process over the years has been evolving year after year. In my journals I find myself being vulnerable and open without restriction. I relate this realization of reflection and vulnerability being imperative to the field of social work for many reasons, one being the fact that in the practice of social work both co-participants, client and therapist, have to be vulnerable enough to build rapport and understand each other. As a social worker, having the ability to understand my experiences and make sense of what is happening in my life and why it might be happening is an essential skill to have. This level of self-awareness gives me the strength to be vulnerable enough with my client to connect on a deeper level, and it gives me an advantage to serve my clientele to the best of my ability.

The practice of reflection has assisted in my evolving into the woman I am still becoming today. I believe that reflection helps me to put my own life and my experiences into perspective. I consider the instruction that I am receiving in various courses, specifically Critical Race Theory, and the concepts that I am learning, such as institutional power, social power, and social justice. I think about these concepts and how they affect my life, having an understanding of these has allowed me to shift my perspective on how I look at systems of oppression and how they shape my life and the life of the students I currently serve at my field placement. Reflection has definitely adjusted the way I will practice social work. The evidence based theories and models that frame and define the practice of social work are necessary, however I believe that true reflection calls for social workers to be culturally competent. The practice of reflecting is permitting me to explore how I can start where the client is, how can I break the barriers that could be potential challenges for me in serving the client, how can I focus on empathizing with the client to build stronger rapport, how can I assure the client that I am concerned, perceptive, and understanding to what they are feeling.

In order to do any of these things I must first have a secure sense of who I am and where my potential clients are in regards to their emotional state and what they may be currently experiencing. I believe that taking a more holistic approach in the practice of social work requires an individual to reflect on themselves first in order to best serve the client.

As I go through this program and recall my experience thus far, I am becoming more inspired by the practice of reflexivity. This practice inspires me because I believe that this practice enables social workers to engage in critical self-reflection. This is important especially when I consider what values and goals are important to me as a future social worker. Being able to reflect critically about my background, my behavior, and experiences and how they relate or do not relate to my clients, is the first step to being genuinely self-aware and culturally competent. The values that are the core of social work practice are the same values that I believe in, going through this program and reflecting on how privileged I am compared to the populations I currently serve and will serve in the future, reinforced my passion to make sure that I am not adding directly or indirectly to the disenfranchisement of those individuals living inside the margins society has made. I am an individual that enjoys the luxurious things in life. I do believe that material things are not necessarily what makes people happy, however being in this program I have become so much more humble and I have come to the realization that it is truly the simple things that make individuals happy and feel wanted. It is this kind of reflection about myself and my actions that make me realize that I have to consider every individual that I come in contact with has a story that is much different or maybe even similar to my own. Going through life, before this program I never considered this thought of a person's story as complex. Being naive to the fact that what I see at face value is not the complete story of a person, is what intrigues me more about reflective practice. A person's narrative is so complex for many reasons. Being an individual that has a story that is not on a 'grand scale' of complexity coming from a modern family, I would assume that everyone's life was as stable as my own. However, this is not so, and as I reflect on my own family dynamics and the family dynamics of the population that I serve, I think about the single story, my single story, and what it tells people about me that I have not told them myself.

Practicing social work has allowed me to examine my story and compare it to the one that is already written for me by society. As a practicing social worker I examine my true story and the stories of others I interact with and I am coming to the realization that there are multiple layers to who a person is, and specifically to who I am. Being a black first generation graduate in my family is not only my story as I reflect on the lives of other minority populations that have to endure the labels and misconceptions because of what society wants us to believe about them. Reflecting on my time in this program I have come to understand that people do not focus on another person's story in its entirety, only the single story, the socially constructed version. The problem with that is the single story perpetuates the misconception that those preconceived notions or stereotypes are true and the fact is stereotypes are not untrue, it is that they are incomplete (Adichie, 2009). As I consider this thought about the single story, it inspires me to never disregard a person's history and always acknowledge the multiple layers of their lives because it is those complex layers that make them who they are.

My journey through this social work program has been stimulating, enlightening, very intense and at times discouraging. Nonetheless, being able to engage in courses such as critical race theory has given me the insight and critical thinking skills that will frame my interactions with clients in the future. Although I am confident in knowing that I will pursue the macro sector of social work, this decision will still put me in a position to serve others in a larger capacity. My field work placement has helped me engage in macro and micro practice, which gives me an opportunity to focus on how I am making a positive impact on these students' lives at such a young age. Focusing on this helps me reflect on how I had mentors and a strong family support system that enhanced my emotional stability and reinforced my positive behavior, which allowed me to do well through school. Being involved with these students brings a sense of purpose to my life, which I find to be ironic considering how little interest I had in becoming a teacher or social worker. However, studying about this practice and applying my knowledge to my field placement has been a very gratifying experience, that has caused me to take a look at myself, my story, and my experiences. I am now starting to reevaluate my life, the path I want to take as I continue to pursue a career in social work, and the woman I want to become to my family, my children, my clients, and my community.

My awareness of self has influenced my interaction with clients I have now and will continue to have a great impact on my practice after graduation because I will always consider the individuals in my life who have encouraged me along my journey. These people have given me the skills to grow in every aspect of my life. What has been beneficial for me, such as spiritual growth, patience, mindfulness, and acceptance, may inspire others. Knowing myself will enhance my ability to serve my clients in a more holistic way.

In my own experience I have come to the conclusion that being self-aware is essential in order to understand one's own emotions, triggers, etc. and how to control them. In a professional sense, reflection is just as important because in order to be a leader, manage, and get along with colleagues, one must be aware of such things as well. Achieving self-awareness is a lifelong effort and I strongly believe that it is important in a profession where the goal is to evoke change in the world by enhancing the well-being of others by helping to meet their needs and empower them. Without reflecting on one's self in this profession, the responsibility to be of service to those who are marginalized would be apathetically met. Being in this social work program I have come to understand that personal and professional overlap in a profession like social work. Continuing to reflect on myself, how I am growing, seeing where I can improve, recognizing my strengths and working on my weaknesses will be a life long process. In my beginning of studying self I am charged with taking time and effort to evaluate myself, see where I am going, where I want to be, and what I must do in order to get there. I hope to continue to work toward being the change I want to see in the world, and to keep reflecting on my experiences so that I can inspire others to be their best as I strive to do the same.

References

Adichie, C.N. (2009) 'The danger of a single story,' TED Global. www.ted.com/talks/chi mamanda_adichie_the_danger_of_a_single_story?language=en

10

MY NARRATIVE (ANTHONY CONSTANTINO)

PROFILE

Anthony Constantino is a 38-year-old from Los Angeles, California, who takes an absurdist/existentialist/mindfulness view of life. He would like to see a world with less suffering, sadness, poverty and desperation.

Introduction

In the first sections of the following narrative, Anthony explores his journey into education framed in a rich and densely storied format. His narrative takes a postmodern approach in thinking about understanding people and society generally. The brief story he tells is integrated by social and cultural stories, all of which are expressed in his discussions of self. As I have stated earlier, stories can be interpreted in many different ways; narratives illuminate experiences as readers can discover and make meanings of them. In the end, what we see is that the author has a sense of service to others through his own childhood experiences.

★★★

There were several factors that served as my motivation to enter the social work field. It's best to examine the issues chronologically. As a child who suffered some amount of emotional abuse and trauma, and has spent several years overcoming it, I felt like I had wasted time. I had wasted several underachieving years in community college, wasted several years of my twenties, wasted time in general going through life as an unaware human being. Gradually, as I developed awareness of my lack of development, I felt like I had an obligation to help others who may have been in similar situations. I enjoyed the world of therapy and counseling, of engaging in my own bouts of reflection and contemplation, and I wished to spread this knowledge and experience to others who may have needed it. I saw the massive amounts of sadness and hopelessness pervading the working class life, of emotionally under-developed individuals believing that getting a job, getting married, and having children was the ultimate goal in life, regardless of whether or not they were truly ready to guide and raise a human child. I began to see stunted individuals passing on their faulty belief systems to their children, and I saw how nature did not really care that this was occurring, as long as the species continued. I felt like I had an obligation to try to minimize the perpetuation of this condition.

My goal now is to increase education of humans in general, to reduce the rate of childbirth, to minimize the amount of children unwillingly brought into a world of misery and suffering, to minimize the suffering of living beings as much as possible. My journey through the field of social work education has been interesting, illuminating, redundant, and exasperating. The concept of self-determination seems to be strongly promoted in this field, but I question how much leeway an individual should be given when making decisions that negatively affect themselves or others. I believe in a strong government, in strong oversight of individuals by society, and strong pressure for society to agree upon the best course of action for individuals to take. However, I may support this view partly because I exist in a state that is privileged enough to be in position to dictate behavior to others.

My education has exposed me to many people who seem to express strong emotions when it comes to how they are perceived and treated in this country. These individuals seem to blame ulterior motives by the dominant powers when it comes to why things happen in the world. The postmodern world is not a world of who is right or wrong, better or worse, but a world of who feels insulted, oppressed, discriminated against. This is now a world in which those outside of the dominant power structure no longer believe in the status quo, as they do not seem to believe that it serves their interests. Class discussion, and postmodernism in general, is less about coming to a single, verifiable, unified conclusion, but rather about how multiple conclusions are neither right nor wrong, but are right for each individual. As someone who is highly cerebral, theoretical, philosophical, and intellectual, I have found this approach to be fairly uninteresting and lacking in stimulation, as I am admittedly a fairly unemotional person, but I accept the purpose of it, for if I wish to see progress in society; we must use emotions, as they are an important tool for the facilitation of communication and transference of information. I feel that because of the highly social nature of this program, and the university experience in general, I have improved in my ability to engage in human interaction and find interest in the emotions of others.

Lived experiences of learning and being in the moment with others have made me fairly uncomfortable and impatient, at times, as I am a solution-oriented individual who dislikes spending large amounts of time expressing displeasure with a situation, but would rather quickly find a solution to the problem and solve it. As emotions are important to most people, they spend more time than I do expressing themselves, and I find myself drifting off when I would rather be telling them how they can solve their problem. It seems that, at times, people either find some sort of pleasure in dragging out their discomfort, or just do not have the same ability as myself when it comes to improving one's situation. Hence, I would rather be off on my own rather than be involved with the complaints and frustrations of others, even if it means I must eventually end up with a small social circle.

As to locating myself personally professionally in the social work context, I am undecided as to whether or not I will be able to be productive over a long period of time in the field of social work. I do believe that there are many different ways we can fit into our occupational choice, as humans are a behaviorally diverse species with room for everyone, but I feel like I want to find a way where I can make as large an impact as possible in the shortest amount of time. Ground-floor casework seems like a waste of my talents, as I feel that I have many theoretical ideas to propose, and will most likely end up spreading my ideas on the Internet, at some point. However, I know from my previous employment experiences that all types of people are open to improvement, and people have expressed thanks after listening to my thoughts on certain issues. It's hard to estimate how much of my education I will retain, but it has been a fairly worthwhile endeavor, though I do believe a semester or so could shorten the process.

The world of practice will change depending upon the job that needs to be done. Humans forget things fairly quickly when the tasks are not used in daily life; I am currently focusing on preparing myself for my job by learning as much as possible at the internship. I wish to become a fast and accurate worker who excels at his job, and since my job will essentially be case management, I don't envision using many clinical interventions. Our social work education gave us a jack of all trades experience, macro/mezzo/micro, which is as decent of a preparation as possible for a career in the field. In practice, I will not be allowed to pontificate or theorize; I will be working directly with humans to find solutions to problems. I am excited to see if I am able to adapt to a new, highly social situation enough to be an effective worker, and to see if being exposed to the negative aspects of humanity will affect my attitude and level of interest in my job.

My values are reflected in social work in that I think that a person reaches a certain level of comfort and privilege where it starts to lose its impact. Individuals who have too much comfort and wealth often become their own worst enemy by losing touch with the nature of wealth. Certain studies have shown that the amount of money one person needs to cover the basic levels of happiness is around US\$70,000–80,000 a year; anything above this starts to move into the world of gratuitous, unnecessary wealth that people use to pay for expensive diversions in life. I am an individual who requires very little; I have a slightly Buddhist outlook on life in that I believe that material possessions are overrated, and spiritual and intellectual wealth is far more valuable. Therefore, I believe that we have an obligation to help those who have very little reach a point where they have enough, even at the expense of raising taxes on the wealthy, on individuals who have far more than they could ever find necessary for survival. Far more suffering comes from having very little, rather than from not having millions of dollars, therefore it is our duty to prevent suffering, if we have the ability to do so.

Again, I support the principle of advancing the human race through the reduction of oppression, poverty, suffering, and other social ills. I believe in a global society more than I believe in a society that can be kept separate, defined separately, organized separately, etc. As humanity continues to mix its ethnicities, cultures, and genetics, attempts at segregating ourselves along these demographic lines are futile. As technology advances and the migration of humans increases, it will become harder and harder to attempt to define concepts and events in a concrete manner; eventually, our society will morph and evolve at an incredible pace, faster than most events can be processed and analyzed. My personal value of encouraging people to understand that competition is a non-negotiable force will be expressed in my work when I encourage people to ensure that their focus should be on financial security and promoting the education and stability of their children rather than rushing into having multiple offspring or spending their income on unnecessary items.

The practice of reflection has assisted in my development of personal growth by being part of a constant system of checks and balances, of praxis, as my experiences inform my theories, and my theories inform my style of practice. I wouldn't say that reflection has adjusted my practice much, because as a social worker, I must follow the agreed-upon, evidence-based theories and models that are embraced by the greater social work profession. What it does change, however, is how I react to what I see in the world, and whether I start to become more deeply affected by what I experience. I already have a sense of what I will continue to see throughout my social work career; namely, poverty, trauma, mental illness, and various other negative experiences of society. What will be important is whether I start to let it affect me in an increasingly negative sense. Will my growth be stunted by working in an industry that focuses on meeting people where they are, usually in a state of crisis or chaos?

I am the prototypical straight white male, generally a loner, the one who is used as a scapegoat and target for anti-establishment theories. I find it humorous that most people don't realize that the same generalizations that are used to promote racism are being used to promote anti-majority views. A backlash is already occurring, however, as the postmodern multi-culturalists are thrown into states of confusion when minority police officers abuse minorities, or when a minority president fails to truly make change that his supporters are expecting. On the other hand, I feel thankful for the rise in diversity in the world, as the challenging of minority worldviews has been educational and enlightening, to a good extent. The diversity of ethnicities, gender identities, and other demographics, has certainly made the world more interesting and colorful to me, and made some of my friends happier to find their rights and identities gaining respect and protection that they previously did not possess. My thought is that as long as the blame does not get too intense or personal, I am willing to humor those who think that everything bad in human history started because of straight white men being who they are, rather than with the greedy behaviors of people who just so happened to match these demographic identifiers.

Considering key aspects of my identity, I think society will find that there are drawbacks to being a straight white man, who supposedly possesses the most privilege out of all demographics. If my demographic is at the top of the power structure, the downside is that the top is a lonely place to be, and that even murderous dictators have nightmares of their conquests, with empty souls that cannot be filled by treasure. This is another reason I do not mind things like affirmative action and other policies that seek to 'level the playing field' by demanding results and outcomes which will result in the power of the straight white male being reined in; this demographic does have too much wealth and power, and the world may be a better place by ensuring that some of it is redistributed to those who have very little. The lesson that will be important to learn is that demographics have very little to do with whether a person will end up as good or bad, greedy or generous; there have been, and will be, evil people of all colors, ethnicities, cultures and genders.

My awareness of self influences my practice in the sense that I always keep in mind that what worked for me (self-realization, spiritual growth, mindfulness, acceptance) may work for someone else. This approach can be fairly well-supported with basic deductive and inductive reasoning by examining why humans behave the way they do, how they learn such behavior, the benefits and drawbacks of such behavior, and why the behavior endures over time. In my own experience, I was a human born to two individuals not of my choosing, where I endured trauma, where I had little control over my environment for a large part of my life, where I had to spend several years overcoming such trauma, and these experiences defined who I am and how I approach my interaction with other people. I don't believe that my 'self' is necessary to be an effective social worker; the rules, policies and procedures are created for us, so I feel that my 'self' is more important as it pertains to how I am affected by my practice.

11

A GIFT TO A STUDENT SOCIAL WORKER (ANNA MARIE MONCK)

PROFILE

Anna Marie Monck worked as an Operations Manager for a large corporate business before attending Canterbury Christchurch University, England, where she received a first-class honors degree in social work in 2015. She is currently living in Kent, England, with her partner and two children, whilst working as a frontline child protection social worker for a local authority.

Introduction

In this final narrative, Anna considers the *Alice's Adventures in Wonderland* story as an analogy for her journey through social work education. Her motivation began with a simple desire to help others, and interactions with others along the way became her entrée into self-inquiry and is described as a 'light bulb' moment. As Anna's practice story reveals, looking back through practice experiences, journaling played a key role in writing and learning about the person she is today. These writings tell us about the lived reality of self gaining insights and meaning in practice as ongoing movement and development. What we see are learning experiences in every interaction. This is a gift; how we receive and use these gifts is where the self reveals self in relationship to others. For Anna, narrative and lived experiences are a learning tool and reflection becomes the seat of continuous learning and understanding as each gift unfolds in new and different ways.

★★★

When I think about my journey through the social work degree I am reminded of the children's story, *Alice's Adventures in Wonderland*. Alice falls into a hole and from there on she embarks on a journey that changes her forever and that is exactly what happened during my time at university. I became more aware, more confident, brighter; more alive even. I am motivated and passionate, more so than ever before. During Alice's journey through Wonderland she meets some interesting characters each with their own story, their own problems and needs, and each character has something to teach Alice. Each of these interactions develops Alice's understanding of herself and this was mirrored throughout the degree program. I had many interactions that taught me something about myself, some obvious, like light bulbs switching on suddenly, while others remained subtle, less tangible; this learning took longer to understand and came later in the program. Alice had a white rabbit that would keep her on track through her journey, occasionally pointing her in a direction or prompting a choice of pathway. Whilst on my journey I too would have a metaphorical white rabbit, but this job would change hands like a baton in a relay race. Firstly, I had an academic tutor, then a placement supervisor followed by a practice educator in my final year. These people would offer support and direction and these relationships were all different and all vital in my journey. But just like these important people, there would also be several significant moments during the period of training that would have a huge impact on my understanding of the role of social worker and how I might undertake such a role. The journey through the social work degree program has changed me, developed me and now I am emerging from the hole a completely different person to the one that entered three years ago. I am now a newly qualified social worker working in frontline child protection armed with a marvelous story of a journey that began in 2012 with a simple desire to help others.

The single most significant moment in the first year of study came from a lecturer and in a single moment any doubt I had previously harbored about whether this was the profession for me slipped away and was replaced with passion to succeed. Social work in the UK has a terrible reputation; known as child snatchers or do-gooders, there is little let up from the media. I knew this before I had even decided to apply to university. What I was less aware of was the need for social workers, the difference that a great social worker can make and ultimately the reason for the profession in the first place. This would be my first 'light bulb' moment.

The lecturer walked into the room and cast an eye around taking in each face staring back expectantly. This was the first time this lecturer would teach us and unlike all the other softly spoken, mother like, female lecturers that had preceded, this lecturer was a man; a large, dominant man. He placed his books down on the table and enjoying the silence of the room removed his coat and settled himself on the edge of the desk. Propped by the desk he sat silently until the room was completely uncomfortable, students glancing from one to another; no one dared move. The silence was unbearable. Pointing at one student, he asked a question. When the answer came he moved on to the next question and so on, question after question. It was terrifying. I was so aware of how little we knew as a cohort, with each wrong answer concreting the lack of knowledge. When he stopped asking questions, he quietly began to stroll back and forth at the front of the room, waiting until the silence filled the room. Outside rain hit the skylights and thunder gently rolled on. Suddenly his voice boomed around the room matching the weather outside as he told a story of a young boy that had drowned in a bath by the hands of his own mother. He described the little boy, aged just seven, who loved dinosaurs and telling jokes but who would regularly stumble over the pun and ruin his own jokes. He gave the boy a character. The mother he went on to describe as a mousy women quick to tears whenever the volatile relationship she shared with the boy's father was mentioned, who spoke warmly and lovingly about her son, and had killed her son to protect him; this was the story she had told the jury. The lecturer had caught the imagination of the whole room; everybody watched, waiting for the next words. This he went on to say could be our case, this seven-year-old living with domestic violence. It's a common story and it could be our job to work with that family, and what he wanted to know was what would we have done to prevent that mother from running that last bedtime bath.

The sheer power of that statement singularly made me realize just how important the role of social work was. That little boy, who even to this day I am unsure as to whether he was somebody's real case or a fictional story used as a learning motivator, had lit something in me. From then on I gorged on academic journals, I breathed books and slept on debates of ethical dilemmas. I had realized the type of social worker I wanted to be. I no longer had a simple desire to help people but I wanted to support people to prevent that drowning; later I would learn from the same lecturer that sometimes it might just be enough to know that even when you can't stop the unthinkable from happening, then at least know that you can hold your head high and say you did everything possible to prevent it. The most important thing that thundery day would teach me was that I was a social worker – cut me open and written through my veins like a stick of rock is the title social worker. It took over my life in the most glorious way.

During the second year of the degree program we would attend 100 days of placement within a non-statutory setting. I was assigned a secondary school for children aged 11–17 as my placement. I was unclear as to what to expect in such a setting. When I attended school as a young child there were no social workers on site. There was a clear divide between education and social well-being. We went to school to learn and that was the sole provision provided. I left school back in 2000, just as New Labour were settling in and turning their focus to a child 'readiness for learning.' More and more educational settings were becoming involved in the children's home lives – providing respite for some, and for others a whole wealth of problems. This has continued through to contemporary times, with many schools employing an on-site social worker.

Sitting in a classroom prior to the first day of placement the lecturer and an off-site education officer were talking to us about our expectations, fears and anxieties for our time away from the university. Because I was unclear as to the role of social workers in a school, I had minimal expectations but I certainly had anxieties and fears. Having been a slightly mature student, being in my thirties and having experienced workplaces, I worried about office politics, about fitting in and about the day to day expectations that the placement setting would have on me. It was planned that I would start the week before Christmas and this would be my induction week, then after a two week break I would return and commence my placement. Whilst I worried about fitting in and the day to day role, I had overlooked the biggest learning curve I would undergo that year – coping with the emotions that go with a job that places us at the core of the worst things that a human can do to another human. I knew that this placement was going to test me, I just wasn't sure how.

Right from the offset I kept a journal. To begin with I filled it with research about child development theories relating to secondary school aged children, research I had done into the local area and the school. For instance, I knew that the school had over 1,000 students registered but that these children traveled from nearby towns and villages, bringing children from the poorest areas in Kent and some of the wealthiest together in one school. I knew that several years ago a massive campaign had been launched by the school to safeguard the children against the traffic of the local roads after several children had been injured, with one fatality. This research was vital for several reasons. Firstly it boosted my practice knowledge, but more importantly it provided me with confidence. Confidence was something that I have struggled with throughout the course.

The first day of the degree my fellow cohort were all discussing their experiences and knowledge of social work and I felt completely out of place. Prior to the course I had been a business manager for ten years and had no clue about the health and social care sector. Many of the other students had studied social sciences at school, such as psychology or sociology, whereas I had studied the arts. I had never thought of myself as intelligent and considered my only skills to be working with people in the broadest of senses. I didn't fully understand the role of a social worker and spent the first few weeks really considering whether this was the right course for me. But something pushed me forward and with each lecture and each essay I realized that 'working with people' meant so much more and that my natural skills in this area grew as I understood how to use these skills and what they meant. I had a desire to be great, I wanted to be the best possible social worker I could be. Each success developed my confidence and by the time placement came around I felt knowledgeable enough that I could give it a really good go. But I also knew that this placement was make or break. Not only would it be assessed for fitness to practice but also it would do something to me. During my time on placement I would align my personal identity to that of the professional. And it was this combination of confidence in self and growing professional identity that made my placement an incredible learning experience. One particular incident would educate me in a way that could never be taught in the classroom. This experience drew on me as a person, my emotions and my understanding of the world. I wrote about it in my journal ...

Sitting in an office, chairs filling every tiny space, the windows steaming from the heat. I glance over at the 14-year-old girl, the focus of everyone's attention. Head down, playing with her hands, wringing them, as tears roll quietly down her face. As the words leave her mouth the room inhales in unison, the only sound is the police officer scribbling intently. 'He raped me'; words that changed the world for everyone in that room. Her mother devastated, shame, guilt and pain visibly taking over the girl, the teacher she confided in, is in a far off place, one where perhaps her own child is sitting in this room, the police officer's job load just doubled as the seriousness of the crime becomes more apparent, and then there's me. A student social worker, my role in such a situation unclear, my mind is unfocused. I want to cry. I bite back the lump in my throat and begin to concentrate on the professionals in the room. I watch how they angle themselves to respect personal space whilst maintaining a position that allows them to observe the girl. I listen to the careful selected words the police officers use, the paralanguage creates the heartbeat that the room syncs with. Calmness settles over the room. I observe how the teacher's attention is completely on the mother, watching as her hand slides into her daughter's. We're a group, all women, united with shared involvement in this girl's experience.

The scene described is one I have reflected upon many times. It was a few days after this meeting, in supervision, that I explored the emotional impact of what I had experienced in that room. There were many feelings I needed to explore but the overriding theme provided me a deep learning curve that changed all future experiences and reflection processes. It was one that I was unprepared for, unconsidered in the classroom. Guilt. Guilt infiltrated every reflection, every conversation, and every thought process. As a student these interactions, the service user narrative and their lived experience becomes our learning tool. I went home at the end of my working day and continued with my life, with preparing dinner and other mundane daily routines; meanwhile a family was picking up the pieces from that meeting. There would be no release from their pain that night. I wrote extensively about the young girl and theorized about the impact of the rape, considered literature and research, reflected on emotions and boundaries. Essentially this one experience fortified huge development in my professional capability and knowledge but for that young girl it was life changing and herein developed the guilt I felt. In supervision I was assured that every experience would provide learning. Even when professionals are experienced the learning never stops. I was reminded of the power we have as individuals to learn from each other. The biggest learning I had whilst on placement last year stemmed from this one experience; that every interaction is a gift. How we receive and use that gift will be as personal as the delivery of the gift would be.

This learning permutated the final year of study; it acted like a muse and inspired me to grasp each incident and critically analyze everything because what I had learnt whilst sitting in that room was that 'service users' are real people who don't get to go home and cook dinner, read bedtime stories and switch off from whatever the crisis they may be experiencing, they go home and cook dinner and carry the pain with them and as a professional we are tasked with doing the very best we can for those people. They are real people. This is my mantra. Any disconnect from study and practice was no longer there in that final year. Having experienced real conversations, real crisis, real emotion the classroom teaching became more alive. Furthermore, having tested the emotional boundaries, I had discovered my coping techniques, I had learnt that it was okay to go home and switch off but also when that became difficult I could reflect on it successfully with my supervisor; it didn't make me weak, it didn't make me 'not ready,' it was a reality and it was healthy.

When the final year placement came about, I no longer worried about my confidence because armed with a professional identity and a passion for that profession I was ready to undertake the role of student social worker one last time and was excited to receive the gifts that each interaction would deliver. Interestingly during this final year I was working with child protection with a local authority and therefore the cases I experienced were often the more extreme cases of neglect or abuse, but my focus when reflecting on these cases considered quite specific incidents that to others would seem mundane and unimportant but in these I would learn about me as a practitioner. The big emotions, the big questions and the big topics were discussed with my team, my manager or during supervision and would provide good learning opportunities but it was the bread and butter, the little things that would provide strong learning for me, encouraging the critical reflection that my lecturers had spoken about time and time again.

> I had accompanied a senior practitioner to a service user's home to inform that a date was set for court and to share the documentation required when the local authority seeks an interim care order on a child. It was not this encounter with the young mother but the one that would follow that I would learn so much from. It was the following morning and as the doors to the office opened to the public the young mum presented herself to reception in seeking some time with the social worker. The social worker asked if I would join her in going to reception to speak with the service user. My role was purely observational. The reception area is a large open planned area and is shared with other local authority departments. Understanding of the environment context inferred my reaction to the service user when she became distressed. As soon as we the professionals entered the reception area the service user began to cry. She stood alone, sobbing; visibly shrinking into herself. The senior practitioner spoke clearly to the service user stating there was a room we could use, however the distress of the service user was so great that she didn't respond. My reaction was to place my hand on her back, using my other hand on her arm to guide her towards the door. It is this interaction that I would learn so much from. It raises so many points for discussion; beginning with why had I chosen to physically touch the service user as opposed to using voice? Had I endangered myself by using touch? What meaning could the service user have connected with that act of human contact? What does the

research say about touch in social work? What were the power imbalances with this act? The questions are endless …

This is an extract from my third year placement journal, where I chose to focus on one simple interaction. Later I used this same incident to write an academic essay; here I explored theories to inform and understand, made links to research and critically explored the meaning of this interaction for both me but also the service user. Throughout all the academic waffle of such as essay a key theme became apparent: 'the use of self.' The use of self is such an interesting topic as it encompasses what it means to be a social worker. When we enter someone's home we don't go armed with boxes of tools and equipment like a gas repair man might, we don't have hospitals of equipment and medications, we don't have classrooms full of interesting objects or libraries of books – we have ourselves. The knowledge and equipment we have is all encompassed into us. In a lecture very early on in the degree a guest lecturer spoke about a social worker's tool kit. At the time this meant very little to me but as the years passed and my toolbox grew, so too did my understanding of what this meant. I have concluded that for each of us that toolbox is different; yes we may use similar words to describe what might be in there, for example 'theories,' but which theories we carry in there and how we understand them and more importantly how we use them will be completely unique.

I started this reflection with the analogy of *Alice's Adventures in Wonderland*, and that is where I shall end it. My journey has been incredible, with real moments filled with learning, understanding, confusion, highs and lows. It is impossible to summarize this journey. Each time I reflect back I learn something new, I remember something different and I feel differently but also the difficulty in summarizing this journey lies more in the fact that while I may no longer be in the hole, this is a journey I am still traveling. Just like an adult Alice who will look back at her adventures in Wonderland and remember the pleasures of the joy and the little sorrows, I too will look back at my time as a student of social work and remember each gift that was given to me.

12

FINAL COMMENTS

As I write this concluding section, I reflect briefly upon my own experience of writing this work. The twists and turns all blend into feelings that it is almost finished, yet unfinished because there was so much more that could have been written. Some of my thinking as I moved along featured myself as a reviewer: what would I say if I were reviewing this book? What areas were left out and how about what has been written? I reassured myself that I covered such a range of issues and topics, doing well to tie them together in what I hope was a coherent way. This is what happens when you dip your toe into uncharted waters, blissfully moving through sometimes choppy seas.

This book was also about my story and learning through writing more about myself; through the lived experience as well as the multidimensional aspects of narrative in all its forms and guises. One of the important aspects of writing this book was reading and reviewing student narratives. Although I am aware of the different ways in which social work is defined and understood, it was refreshing to read how these different ways shaped social work thinking and practice. Some of the narratives reminded me of my life experiences of working in so called developing countries and social work as a broader outlook, holding social development as a key aspect of professional activities.

Models of reflection and reflective practice took on a moving platform particularly in charting the pathway of social work through social, economic and political trends affecting the profession in so many different ways. In the past, reflective practice with its attachment to individualized understanding of social problems has in part been blamed for moving radical social work to the margins, helped by postmodern ideas and a focus on individualized cultural aspects of living at the expense of structural issues, thereby slowly diminishing and pushing out social justice and income inequality agendas. Fook (2010), amongst others, folded postmodern ideas in with reflective practice to push through critical social work on an individualized and structural platform. Through writing this book, I found myself reflecting more about personal and professional aspects of my life and life story. This was both a positive and sometimes difficult experience, particularly reflecting upon times best forgotten. Reflection was something that I engaged in but called something else, such as meditation, or experienced hiking in the wilderness where complete peace and silence echoed around me. I can understand authors who are unsure about all the aspects of reflection, as just as meditation and mindfulness can have so many different meanings, I see, just like Johns (2010), that it is a journey, one in which we move through different pathways that have multiple meanings and understandings.

Narrative research

Qualitative research has evolved since its beginnings, moving along through various 'moments' or 'turns' when new trends were spurred and new methods emerged. Narrative research is one of those trends, described as a 'turn' as postmodern influences opened up alternative ways to understand the social world in all its multiple dimensions. The sociology of everyday life and emotions helped in attracting research about hitherto hidden or neglected areas of study. All these trends have provided closer links with the humanities and cultural theories and practice. This is where interest in narrative has grown in the public imagination, through the media where everyday lives come to life as people tell their stories, represented in reality and drama programs. Some of these stories draw audiences in. I know I love 'Life below zero' – a reality program about people living in the wilds of Alaska. I am enthralled by their stories of living in this terrain, mostly isolated and having to fend for themselves through hunting and fishing. This is just one aspect of storytelling and narrative. The developments towards self-inquiry in research hold promise in bringing all aspects of the research process to bear with opportunities to tell stories of lived experiences. Narrative opens up a way of thinking about experiences in a collaboration between researcher and participants over time and place in social interaction. Taking reflection along this path enables new insights or learning about experiences and the research process itself.

References

Fook, J. (2010) 'Beyond reflective practice: reworking the "critical" in critical reflection'. In H. Bradbury, N. Frost, S. Kilminster and M. Zukas (eds), *Beyond reflective practice: new approaches to professional lifelong learning*, London: Routledge, pp. 37–51.

Johns, C. (2010) *Guided reflection: a narrative approach to advancing professional practice*, Oxford: Wiley.

INDEX

accountability 32, 60
Alice's Adventures in Wonderland analogy
  130–1
anti-oppressive practice (AOP) 46
anti-racist and anti-discriminatory practice
  9–10, 20, 46, 47
Anzaldua, G. 82, 83, 87
artistry of practice 36
assessment 32, 33
auto-ethnography 70–1
autobiography 67–70

backgrounds: author 13–15; podcasts of
  student 21–4; student social workers
  82–3, 89–90, 98–9, 113–15, 117,
  118–20, 125–6, 133
Bailey, R. 44
Bochner, A. 70
body, in social and political contexts 39–40
Brake, M. 44
Bruner, J. 66, 67

California State University, Dominguez
  Hills (CSUDH) 7, 9, 19, 24, 81,
  112, 118
Cant, R. 55, 59
care 57–8
careers advice, discriminatory 16
casework, changing approaches to 32
childhood studies 68–70
children's voices 68, 69
codes of ethics 31, 37, 91
Combs, G. 42

competency-based learning: as a measure of
  assessment 32; weaknesses of 32–3
conferences with supervisors 109
Constantino, A. 125–9
Correa, V. 81–7
critical race theory 6, 45, 46–7, 86, 115–16,
  122, 123
critical reflection 25, 34, 35; challenges in
  teaching 11; Fook's approach to 48–9;
  learning from the detail 135–6
critical social work 9–10, 43; Fook's
  postmodern model of reflective practice
  and 47–9, 137–8; influences on early 44
critical theory: postmodern encounters with
  social work, reflection and 43–6;
  reflective practice, postmodernism and
  38–43
critical thinking 66; reflection and 34
cultural identity: reclaiming of Mexican 84;
  suppression of 82, 83–4
cultural studies 25, 67
culturally diverse communities, working
  with 90, 91–5
cultures of social work 79

definitions of social work 77
demographics, changing 10, 128
dialogue, empowering elements of 65–6
discourse 41–2, 49; of 'good' and 'evil' 95;
  of Hindu majoritarianism 89, 94–5
discrimination: author's experiences of
  14–15, 16, 17–18; everyday experiences
  of 47; student experiences of 84–6, 113,

120; towards Muslims in Hindu India 89, 94–5
discursive power 93, 94
diversity: complexity of contemporary 10, 128; rhetoric of 86; super 10

Ellis, C. 6, 12, 13, 70, 71
embodied knowledge 39
emotional: impact of work 133, 134; intelligence 50; labor 50; resilience 51, 128, 135; restraint 101, 107; work and reflective practice 49–51
emotions: discussing of 126–7; in research practice 62, 71
empowerment 11, 17, 26, 114, 115, 117; Solomon's model of 17; strategies of women of color 58–9; through dialogue 65–6
ethnic diversity 10
ethnic identities 45, 115
everyday experiences of discrimination 47
evidence-based practice 33, 60
exchange project, virtual student-to-student 19–21; aims and objectives 19–20; learning experiences 20–1; podcasts 20, 21–4; session times 20; setting up 19
experience, different kinds of 56–7
experiential knowledge 12, 36, 56–9, 67
experimental research 60–1, 71

false beliefs 66
feminism 23, 30, 46, 47, 57, 58
fieldwork placements: challenges of 107; child protection 135–6; with culturally diverse communities 91–4; developing reflective practice in India 99–103; feelings of helplessness in 108–9; learning from the detail 135–6; learning practical skills through 107–8, 110; link between theory and practice 99–101, 103, 106–7, 108, 109; micro and macro practice of 123; with recovering drug addicts in India 108; school social worker 121, 123, 132–3; in slums of Delhi 107–8
Fook, J. 4, 11, 34, 41, 44, 47, 48, 49, 137
Foucault, M. 41, 44, 92, 93
Freedman, J. 42
Freire, P. 65–6

guilt, feelings of 134

Higgs, J. 55, 59, 62
higher education: experiences as outsiders in 15–16, 17–18, 120 *see also* social work education programs

Hochschild, A.R. 50
Holland, S. 69
human rights, ethical research committed to 63
Humphries, B. 63

identity 26; cultural 82, 83–4; ethnic 45, 115; evolving of a multifaceted Chicana Mexican-American 82–5, 87; frontier 90; moving locations and changed 89, 90–1; multiple, interesected 82–5, 87, 113, 115, 117; podcasts of student 21–4; postmodern 57; professional 35, 89, 94–5, 133; restrictions of 110–11; social institutions shaping perceptions of 39; stereotypical 85, 120, 128–9; of straight white male 128–9
indigenous social work 45–6
International Federation of Social Workers (IFSW) 19, 37, 77
international social work 18–20; Frida Svensson's journey to 98–104; variations and local contexts 78–9
intersectionality 40, 45, 46, 86–7, 89–90, 115
Ixer, G. 32, 33

Johns, C. 4, 7, 9, 12, 26, 33, 47, 50, 62, 65, 66, 68, 138
Jones, N. 118–24
journaling 121, 133–4

knowledge: in action 36; defining 60; embodied 39; experiential 12, 36, 56–9, 67; narrative as forms of 66–7; and power 39, 41–2; social construction of 41; ways of knowing 41, 56–9

language 41, 91, 93
LeCroy, C. 77, 78
life stories 24–5, 72, 78; author's 11–18 *see also* narrative; student narratives
lived experience 47, 56, 57; of culturally diverse communities 91–3; as a learning tool 93, 134; narrative and 4, 7, 24–5, 57, 66–7; places to study 70; of women of color 58–9
Llewellyn, C. 62

Marxist theory 44
media portrayals of social work 32, 131
models of reflection 32, 33, 35–7, 47–9, 137–8
Monck, A.M. 130–6

Morley, C. 11
motivations to study social work 8, 13, 77,
   77–8, 86, 89–90, 94, 121, 125–6, 127–8,
   132; and doubts of others over choice
   110–11; podcasts of student 21–4

narrative: author's 11–18; auto-ethnography
   70–1; autobiographical 67–70; children's
   68–70; concept of 4; connecting
   self-reflection and 25–7; as form of
   knowledge 66–7; of historical figures 67;
   inquiry 68, 70–1; interdisciplinary
   application 67, 68; and lived experience
   24–5, 57, 66–7; local 40; postmodern
   influences on interpretation of 57; of
   professions 25; research 5, 64–7, 138;
   social 25; and storytelling 24, 25, 26;
   women's 57 *see also* student narratives
Naruka, Y. 105–11

Oprah Winfrey Show 25
'other' 47, 120; in different locations and
   contexts 89, 90–1; in dominant western
   discourse of social work 90–6
outsider, sense of being an 15, 17, 65, 83

Patil, T. 88–97
personal stories 5, 6, 25; of author 11–18; in
   changing social and political contexts
   64–5; listening to other people's 65;
   sharing podcasts in student-to-student
   exchange project 20, 21–4
Pickering, M. 56
Plummer, K. 64, 65
podcasts in student-to-student exchange
   project 20, 21–4
postcolonial theory 45–6
postmodern identities 57
postmodernism 126; critical race studies and
   45; critical race studies (CRS) and 46–7;
   critical theory and reflective practice
   38–43; encounters with social work,
   critical theory and reflection 43–6;
   influence on interpretation of narratives
   57; local narratives 40; model of critical
   social work and reflective practice 47–9,
   137–8
power: in creation of knowledge 39;
   discursive 93, 94; and knowledge 41–2;
   modern 42; redistribution of 129
practice: fieldwork a bridge between theory
   and 99–101, 103, 106–7, 108, 109; gap
   between theory and 9, 10, 31, 46
professional development 17, 20, 31, 33,
   100, 101, 103

professional education: and reflective
   practice 31; response to international
   social work 19; and trends in approach
   31–4
professional identity: development 89, 94–5,
   133; reflective thinking an element in 35

qualitative research 55–6, 59–60, 63–4, 66;
   new areas of 60–2
quantitative research 55, 59–60

racism 15, 47; author's experiences of 14–
   15, 16, 17; definitions of 45; everyday 47;
   towards African Americans 115, 120; at
   university 120
radical social work 44, 137
reality television 24
reflection: in action 34–5; connecting
   narrative and 25–7; in context of social
   work 36–7; critical 11, 25, 34, 35, 48–9;
   models of 32, 35–7, 47–9, 137–8;
   postmodern encounters with social work,
   critical theory and 43–6; and self-
   awareness 30, 33, 34, 48, 49, 50 *see also*
   self-reflection
reflective practice 3–4, 137–8; adjusting
   theories through 128; artistry of 36;
   author's early engagement with 17–18;
   background in social work 31–3; critical
   theory, postmodernism and 38–43;
   debate on place in social work practice
   33; defining 33–4; and emotional work
   49–51; field supervisor feedback and
   development of 89, 91, 92, 93–4; in
   fieldwork in India 99–103; Fook's model
   47–9, 137–8; key learning strategy in
   development of professional education
   31; knowledge in action at core of 36;
   narrative inquiry as 65, 68; in placement
   in Australia 91–5; skills for 30, 36–7
reflexivity 35, 122
religion 83, 114
report writing, fieldwork 110
research: auto-ethnography 70–1; childhood
   studies 68–70; creative inquiry 61;
   emotional experiences in 62, 71; ethical
   63; as experience 56; framing of questions
   62; historical influences on social work
   59–60; narrative 5, 64–7, 138; qualitative
   55–6, 59–60, 63–4, 66, 138; qualitative,
   new areas of 60–2; quantitative 55,
   59–60; relationship between social work
   and 55; social justice and 63–4; voice of
   researcher 6, 61–2, 70–1; and ways of
   knowing 56–9; writing of 61–2

Said, E. 45, 93
Schön, D. 3, 31, 33, 35, 36, 37
schooling: of author 14, 16; of student
    social workers 83–4, 85, 98–9, 106,
    113–14, 120
self, dissociation of 107
self-awareness: and ability to empathize with
    others 101; and effect of presence on
    others 101–2; and influence on
    interactions with clients 121–2, 124,
    129; journeys of 84–6, 88–97; and
    reflection 30, 33, 34, 48, 49, 50; and
    vulnerability 121–2
self-determination 58, 100, 126
self-esteem 83, 84
self-inquiry 62, 65, 68, 70–1, 138
self-reflection 86, 115; autobiographical 68;
    avoiding 112–13; connecting narrative
    and 25–7; importance to social work of
    121–3; key to helping marginalized and
    oppressed populations 116–17
self, use of 31, 117, 136
Sewell, L. 112–17
social change: postmodern explanations 40;
    social work and 38, 44, 49, 65, 77, 78;
    student narratives on social work and
    108–9, 111, 115, 127
social constructionism 14, 41, 67, 99, 102,
    115, 123; in the toy aisle 119–20
social justice 32, 43, 44, 46; narrative
    research and 63–4
social work education programs 31–4; in
    Australia via doctoral studies in sociology
    89–90; Chicana/Latina studies, journey
    via 85; critique of 126, 127; Elementary
    Education training, journey via 106;
    Indian experience 106–7, 109–10;
    learning experience, journey of 130–6;
    self-doubt of mature student entering
    114–15; Swedish experience 99, 103 see
    also fieldwork placements

Solomon, B. 17
storytelling 24, 25, 26, 64, 66
student narratives 6, 8–9, 66, 77–80;
    Anna Marie Monck 130–6; Anthony
    Constantino 125–9; Frida Svensson
    98–104; Layla Sewell 112–17; Nicole
    Jones 118–24; Tejaswini Patil 88–97;
    Vanessa Correa 81–7; Yogita Naruka
    105–11
superdiversity 10
supervisors: conferences with 109; feedback
    in development of reflective practice 89,
    91, 92, 93–4
Svensson, F. 98–104

technical rationality 36
The Call to Social Work 78
theory: fieldwork a bridge between practice
    and 99–101, 103, 106–7, 108, 109; gap
    between practice and 9, 10, 31, 46;
    reflecting on social work and use of
    different 102–3
touch 135–6
trends in social work approaches
    31–4
Tronto, J. 57, 58

values 37–8, 100–1, 122, 127–8
voices 12; listening to children's 68, 69;
    marginalized 40, 41, 56–7; personal
    narrative 6, 25; of researcher 6, 61–2,
    70–1
vulnerability 121–2

wealth distribution 127–8
western models of social work 44; critique
    of 90–1, 91–5
women of color: empowerment of 58–9;
    and practice of care 57–8
writing: developing skills 109, 110; journal
    121, 133–4; style 12–13